PRIMERS

C000142597

Ornament

Ornament

The Politics of Architecture and Subjectivity

ANTOINE PICON

A John Wiley and Sons, Ltd, Publication

© 2013 John Wiley & Sons Ltd

Registered office
John Wiley & Sons Ltd, The Atrium, Southern Gate, Chichester, West Sussex, PO19 8SQ, United Kingdom

For details of our global editorial offices, for customer services and for information about how to apply for permission to reuse the copyright material in this book please see our website at www.wiley.com.

Wiley publishes in a variety of print and electronic formats and by print-on-demand. Some material included with standard print versions of this book may not be included in e-books or in print-on-demand. If this book refers to media such as a CD or DVD that is not included in the version you purchased, you may download this material at http://booksupport.wiley.com. For more information about Wiley products, visit www.wiley.com.

Designations used by companies to distinguish their products are often claimed as trademarks. All brand names and product names used in this book are trade names, service marks, trademarks or registered trademarks of their respective owners. The publisher is not associated with any product or vendor mentioned in this book.

Limit of Liability/Disclaimer of Warranty: While the publisher and author have used their best efforts in preparing this book, they make no representations or warranties with respect to the accuracy or completeness of the contents of this book and specifically disclaim any implied warranties of merchantability or fitness for a particular purpose. It is sold on the understanding that the publisher is not engaged in rendering professional services and neither the publisher nor the author shall be liable for damages arising herefrom. If professional advice or other expert assistance is required, the services of a competent professional should be sought.

ISBN 978-1-119-96594-7 (hardback)
ISBN 978-1-119-96595-4 (paperback)
ISBN 978-1-118-58753-9 (ebk)
ISBN 978-1-118-65832-1 (ebk)
ISBN 978-1-118-58823-9 (ebk)
ISBN 978-1-118-58824-6 (ebk)

Executive Commissioning Editor: Helen Castle
Project Editor: Miriam Swift
Assistant Editor: Calver Lezama

Cover design, page design and layouts by Karen Willcox for aleatoria.com
Printed in Italy by Printer Trento Srl

Cover image © Kalpesh Patel

Contents

Introduction: Architecture as Ornament?   009

Chapter 1: A Problematic Return   017

    The Ornamental Revival in Contemporary Architecture   019

    Textures, Patterns and Topology: A Different Ornament   027

    The Subjective and the Political   047

Chapter 2: Ornament and Subjectivity   059

    The Visage of Architecture   060

    The Architect, between Rules and Invention   062

    Artists, Craftsmen and the Fabrication of Ornament   073

    From Clients to Passers-By   082

    Industrialisation and the Ornamental Impulse   090

    The Ghost of Ornament   097

Chapter 3: Politics of Ornament   103

    From Economics to Politics   103

    Communication and Style   106

    The Power of Architectural Décor   122

Chapter 4: Reinventing the Meaning of Ornament   129

    A New Architectural Subject   129

    Political Uncertainties   144

    Meaning and Symbols   145

Bibliography   157

Index   163

Picture Credits   167

Acknowledgements

A book often begins and develops through a series of conversations.
I would like to thank here Sarah Whiting for her initial suggestion to
write a book on contemporary architectural ornament. I am indebted to
Farshid Moussavi's pioneering research on the subject. Colleagues on
both sides of the Atlantic, Martin Bressani, Preston Scott Cohen, Patricia
Falguières and Hadas Steiner, have helped me to hone the argument
developed here. Alina Payne has graciously lent me one of the very first
published copies of her book *From Ornament to Object*. Reinhold Martin
and Norton Wise have shared with me precious information. My doctoral
students Peter Sealy and Marrikka Trotter have been kind enough to read
parts of this essay. At Wiley, Helen Castle's constant support has proved
invaluable, and Caroline Ellerby has played an essential role in assembling
the illustrations.

My deepest gratitude goes to my colleague Erika Naginski who has read,
criticised and edited this book chapter after chapter.

Introduction
Architecture
as Ornament?

What if architecture were ultimately about ornament? Even décor. In *The Mediation of Ornament*, Islamic art specialist Oleg Grabar proposes to interpret it from this very perspective. 'Good architecture is always meant to be an invitation to behave in certain ways; it always adorns life, and, some exceptions notwithstanding, does not require the emotions surrounding whatever one does in a building, including looking at works of art,' states Grabar, concluding that 'architecture is a true ornament (...). Without it, life loses its quality. Architecture makes life complete, but it is neither life nor art.'[1]

For a designer, there is something profoundly disturbing in the thought that architecture corresponds to neither life nor art, but rather is an ornament for both. The nagging feeling that there might be some truth in this could be partly responsible for the early 20th-century demise of traditional décor, as if the conception of the discipline that it hinted at had become, after centuries of tolerance, all of a sudden unbearable. We will return to Grabar's assertion about architecture, life and art later. Let us begin by acknowledging the return of ornament in contemporary architecture. This return constitutes the subject of the present book.

From professional journals to scholarly texts, it has become commonplace to evoke this reappearance, as if the reluctance of Modernism to recognise the crucial character of adornment were finally about to be overcome. The role played by the computer has likewise been acknowledged. Design

Herzog & de Meuron,
Eberswalde Technical
School Library, 1997.
The building is emblematic
of the return of ornament.
The basis for the facade
prints is photos discovered
by the artist Thomas Ruff.
The repetition of the
pictures plays on the frontier
between representative
and abstract, images and
patterns. Revealingly, the
pictorial character of the
facade is not detrimental
to the strong impression of
materiality conveyed by the
building, to the contrary.

software has enabled architects to play with textures, colours, patterns and topologies in highly decorative ways. However, beyond its evident links with the diffusion of digital tools and culture, the meaning of this evolution remains unclear. What are its long-term implications for architecture? Should one consider that the future of the discipline lies in the design of decorated sheds? Is the reduction of architecture to envelope desirable? One thing is certain: ornament represents a delicate issue.

Today's debates echo problems that have a long history in Western architectural tradition. On the one hand, since the Renaissance, architects have periodically insisted on the need to subordinate ornamentation to the overall organisation of buildings. The Modernist demise of ornament can be interpreted as an extreme form of this desire to keep it in check. On the other hand, ornament has often been seen as holding the key to the foundations of architecture. Again, the Modernist ban may appear a desperate attempt to counteract the disturbing feeling that the discipline could be revolving around the question of décor. This feeling has returned today, accompanied by a mix of apprehension and excitement.

Despite these historical resonances, what we call ornament reveals itself as quite different from what it represented in former times. These differences are analysed in detail in the first chapter of this book. Such a gap could lead to the rejection of the very notion of a return. Nevertheless, elements of continuity between past and present can be found in two threads: the first encompasses subjectivity, the second, politics.

Ornament is designed and fabricated by various individuals, architects, artists and craftsmen. It is meant for another series of individuals, from clients to simple passers-by. Ornamentation cannot be understood without taking into account the various subjects engaged in its production and reception. In chapter 2, we will evoke their respective roles in shaping architectural décor from the Renaissance on, as well as the ambiguities which have accompanied their interventions.

Politics constitutes the other possible link between yesterday and today. Contrary to the message conveyed by the founding fathers of modern architecture, from Adolf Loos to Le Corbusier, traditional ornament was not meant solely for pleasure. It conveyed vital information about the purpose of buildings as well as about the rank of the owners. As such, it participated in the expression of social values, hierarchies and order. In chapter 3, the various aspects of the relations between ornament and politics from the Renaissance to the end of the 19th century will be explored. Despite the fact that this role no longer seems evident in contemporary ornamentation, the question of its relation to the expression of collective values has not disappeared, far from it. As argued in the last chapter of the book, the return of ornament is both about the new type of subjectivity characteristic of the digital age and about the possible contribution of architecture to emerging collective meanings and values. Thus, through the ornamental dimension,

Charles Percier, interior view of a museum, circa 1810.
The drawings of Charles Percier (1764–1838) display remarkable ornamental skills. In his work, there is no clear-cut distinction between décor and architecture. With his associate Pierre François Léonard Fontaine, Charles Percier was one of the main creators of the Empire style, this variant of neo-classicism characteristic of the reign of Napoleon I.

Pl. 89.   ET CHAPITEAUX SYMBOL.   299

Plumes d'Autruche   Feüilles de Palmier.

Pl. 89.   P. 299.

BASES COMPOSÉES et CHAPITEAUX SYMBOLIQUES

Bases and capitals of the French order designed by Claude Perrault and of the order used for the Temple of Jerusalem, after Augustin-Charles d'Aviler, *Cours d'Architecture*, 1691. A revealing example of the connection between ornament and politics. On the left, the attempt by French 17th-century architectural theorist Claude Perrault to invent a French order for the Louvre Palace; on the right, the capital of the order used at the Temple of Jerusalem, according to a 16th-century reconstitution. In a variation on the Composite order, Perrault uses ostrich feathers instead of acanthus leaves to express the lightness of his proposed order.

we propose here a reflection on the political and social agency of the architectural discipline beyond its much-discussed contribution to issues such as sustainability. Because we still bear the imprint of Modernist prejudices, we display a tendency to consider the performativity of décor as less important than structural or energetic behaviour. But as French poet Paul Valéry famously noted, nothing is actually deeper than the surface, the skin.[2] Once again, ornament could well hold the key to core architectural issues.

Although the very notion of return seems to imply a strong historical dimension, it has not always been studied from this perspective. Beyond superficial references to John Ruskin or Gottfried Semper, its interpreters have almost exclusively focused on what is happening today with the aid of digital tools, without paying much attention to the genealogies linking past and present. In sharp contrast with the enrolment of history by Postmodernism, this presentist attitude is actually a general feature of today's architectural debate. Published in 1978, Rem Koolhaas's *Delirious New York* was, in fact, one of the last major theoretical contributions based on an innovative mobilisation of architectural and urban history.[3] Until recently, the historical dimension was also quite limited in the study of the digital revolution, even if scholars such as Mario Carpo or Reinhold Martin had explored its connection to former episodes ranging from the invention of the printing press during the Renaissance to the cybernetic turn of the 1950s and '60s.[4] Presentism still reigns supreme in sustainability studies, despite the vernacular precedents to the quest for energy-efficient behaviour.

John Ruskin, Abstract Lines, plate from *The Stones of Venice*, vol 1, 1851.
For Ruskin, abstract lines, derived from nature, are the first constituents of ornament. The plate shows various lines at very different scales, from the profile of a glacier in the Alps (ab) to the curve of a branch of spruce (h). His sensitivity to the dynamic behaviour of natural elements seems to announce the contemporary interest in flows, variations and modulations, one of the sources of the return of ornament.

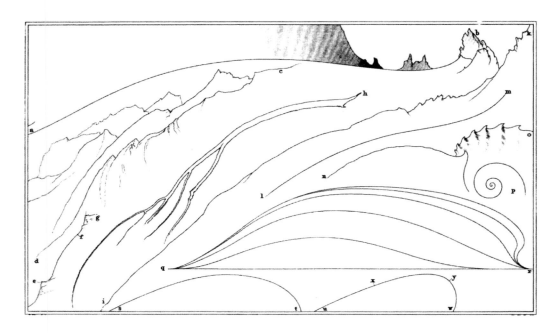

The time has come to break with this attitude, and ornament provides perhaps one of the best opportunities to do so. The opportunity comes not so much from a straightforward continuity between past and present as from an intricate, almost labyrinthine set of similarities and dissimilarities between what was once called ornament and the type of décor that now lies before our eyes. Contrary to what one might imagine, history reveals itself more productive when the present does not appear as a mere extension of the past but seems, rather, to stem from a complex reinterpretation of some of its elements, a reinterpretation in which continuities and discontinuities need to be carefully sorted and weighted. The co-founder in the 1930s of the renowned group of French historians – the Annales School – Marc Bloch once declared that history must convey an 'imperious sense of change', and the complexity of the relations between past and present is one of the preconditions to fulfil this mission.[5] Simultaneously, the realisation that things have indeed changed must come with an impression of déjà-vu, which suggests underlying threads relating former historical moments to present-day issues. It is only when it explores this mix of change and permanence that history carries lessons. This is what we have attempted here when grappling with the return of architectural ornament. This book is as much about the operativity of history as about the agency of architecture.

Architectural agency and historical operativity are actually interconnected. To put it in simpler terms, the practice of architecture needs the lessons of history, even if the need is felt less acutely at certain periods than at others. Again, the ties between architecture and history have been at a low ebb for the past two decades. Why this enduring though fluctuating link? The answer probably lies in the strong self-referential character of the architectural discipline. At the time when the doctrine of imitation still prevailed in the arts, that is until the mid-18th century, theorists often remarked that whereas painting and sculpture imitated nature, architecture had a propensity to imitate itself. Architecture is partly based on the meditation of its former achievements as well as shortcomings. Modernism did not break with this self-reflexive stance, and now modern architecture itself has become a legacy that must be reinvested with new meaning.

One could also suggest that architecture is perhaps more accurately described as a tradition than as a discipline. A tradition, a living tradition that is, is not something static. At each stage, it implies handing down but also loss, the price paid for moving forward. Sometimes a dimension considered as constitutive of the theory and practice can become rapidly obsolete while others are maintained and even accentuated. At other times, long-forsaken or at least neglected aspects can be retrieved or reinvented. Both scenarios have applied to ornament. It almost disappeared during the first decades of the 20th century. It is now making a surprising comeback.

History plays a fundamentally critical role when exploring this mix of loss and transmission. Part of its task consists in deconstructing the disciplinary illusion of an architecture which would have steadfastly pursued the same objectives throughout its evolution. The goals of the discipline have changed, just like some of its key dimensions and notions. For instance, before the advent of Modernism, ornament represented a fundamental dimension of architectural design, while space was not considered as such. We are currently observing a dramatic reversal of this situation, with the return of ornament and the simultaneous decline of the Modernist obsession with space.

There is no disillusionment without the attempt to re-create simultaneously new enchantment. When some myths are dispelled, others almost immediately replace them, so strong is the desire to believe, hence Walter Benjamin's famous characterisation of 19th-century capitalism, despite its desire to be eminently rational, as 'a reactivation of mythical forces'.[6] Behind the critical assessment of transmission and loss, and despite the conscious attempt to deconstruct some of the grand claims of the architectural discipline, history reveals itself deeply permeated by the desire to identify or at least catch a glimpse of what could remain untouched by the flow of historic conditions. This is where its agenda meets with the ambition of theory. Part of the magic of architecture lies in the suggestion that an unmovable core exists beneath its ever-changing theories and modes of practice. The role of history is to serve this magic by touching on it lightly, instead of producing normative statements, which usually belong to the category of disciplinary illusions. At the same time, many buildings remain foreign to architecture – in that they are not designed by architects and have little relation to architectural ideals – as if architecture were something added to construction, like a garment, make-up or even perfume, the most volatile of all body adornments. This troubling fact hints at another feature of the discipline: a gratuity and instability in sharp contrast with the overt striving of architecture for permanence. Gratuity and instability are also essential for architectural magic to operate. The ornamental dimension lies on the very border that separates enchantment and disillusion, magic and rationality. It makes architecture vibrate, hence the recurring analogy made with music. On the one hand, ornament points towards permanence by helping to outline the overall organisation of a building. On the other hand, it displays disruptive tendencies leading to the blurring of this organisation. To put it in slightly different terms, ornamentation always marks a threshold; it appears as a structure of exchange rather than as a static entity. This is where the nagging feeling that we mentioned earlier re-emerges: could adornment, décor, tell us something absolutely essential about architecture, despite the Modernist attempt to make us believe the contrary? This feeling ultimately represents what this book is about.

References

1 Oleg Grabar, *The Mediation of Ornament* (Princeton: Princeton University Press, 1992), p 193.
2 Paul Valéry, 'L'Idée Fixe', 1931, in *Oeuvres*, t 2 (Paris: Gallimard, 1960), pp 195–275, p 215 in particular.
3 Rem Koolhaas, *Delirious New York: A Retroactive Manifesto for Manhattan* (New York: Oxford University Press, 1978).
4 Mario Carpo, *Architecture in the Age of Printing: Orality, Writing, Typography, and Printed Images in the History of Architectural Theory* (Cambridge, MA: MIT Press, 2001); Reinhold Martin, *The Organizational Complex: Architecture, Media, and Corporate Space* (Cambridge, MA: MIT Press, 2003).
5 Marc Bloch, 'Que Demander à l'Histoire', *X-Crise*, no 35, February 1937, pp 15–22, p 16 in particular.
6 Walter Benjamin, *The Arcades Project* (Cambridge, MA: Harvard University Press, 1999), p 391.

1

A Problematic Return

Over the past 10 to 15 years, ornament or rather ornamental practice has made a spectacular return in architecture. This return has taken diverse forms. The repeated silkscreened photographs used by Herzog & de Meuron at the Eberswalde Technical School Library (1997) differ from the coloured cladding of Sauerbruch Hutton's Boehringer Ingelheim Pharmacological Research

Evan Douglis, Choice Market café in Brooklyn, 2010.
In complete contrast with the straightforward floor, walls and furniture, the intricate decoration of the ceiling is not only reminiscent of Baroque or Rococo, it also plays out along the porous border between refinement and kitsch.

Sauerbruch Hutton,
Boehringer Ingelheim
Pharmacological Research
Laboratories, Biberach,
Germany, 2002.
The ornamental character
lies in the use of a
multicoloured glass cladding.
The presence of operable
glass louvres also contributes
to the animation of the
facade.

Laboratories (2002). Despite their shared fascination for spiralling patterns, Evan Douglis's baroque ceiling for the Choice Market café in Brooklyn (2010) follows principles that have nothing to do with those mobilised for the envelope of Foreign Office Architects' Leicester John Lewis department store (2007).

The Ornamental Revival in Contemporary Architecture

This diversity has made the return of ornament even more striking. Its importance for the architectural discipline has been generally acknowledged by theorists and practitioners. It has been discussed in articles such as Greg Lynn's 'The Structure of Ornament' or Robert Levit's 'Contemporary "Ornament": The Return of the Symbolic Repressed'.[1] It has given birth to books such as Farshid Moussavi and Michael Kubo's *The Function of Ornament* or Andrea Gleiniger and Georg Vrachliotis's *Pattern: Ornament, Structure, and Behavior*, both of which have attempted to draw systematic lessons from this revival.[2]

Foreign Office Architects, John Lewis department store, Leicester, 2007. The swirling décor is produced with four different panels that can be easily combined because they share the same pattern at their edges. The double layer produces a 3D impression. It also enables the building to be more transparent from the inside than the outside. Indeed, the people inside typically look horizontally through the aligned swirls, while passers-by contemplate the facade from below, with the two levels of embroidery creating additional opacity.

To fully grasp the novelty and radical character of this revival, it is necessary to remember how modern architecture had been suspicious of ornament almost from the start. In his famous 1929 essay 'Ornament and Crime', Viennese architect Adolf Loos had disparaged ornament as unnecessary, childish, and even 'criminal' in a sense that will be discussed later in this essay. 'The evolution of culture is synonymous with the removal of ornamentation from objects of everyday use,' declared Loos.[3] Since it claimed to be 'of everyday use', modern architecture tended to discard ornament as an incongruity from the past. Most of its proponents followed Loos when he stated that: 'there is no longer any organic connection between ornament and our culture, ornament is no longer an expression of our culture'.[4] In addition to its attempt to be of everyday use, modern architecture aspired to reconnect with the culture of the age of the machine. In this light also, ornament was doomed as a relic.

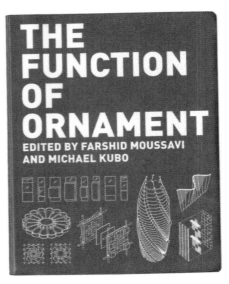

This widespread condemnation did not mean that the ornamental dimension disappeared totally from modern architecture. It remained, for instance, present under different guises in the work of Mies van der Rohe: in the use of precious materials like marble and onyx for the Barcelona Pavilion (1929); or later, at the Illinois Institute of Technology (1958) or the Berlin National Gallery (1968), in the careful design of constructive details somewhat reminiscent of the traditional vocabulary of the orders. Traces of ornamental practices can actually be found in the work of almost every major modern architect, especially after the Second World War, when Modernism finally became culturally dominant. This dominance created the conditions for a new and tacit indulgence towards neo-ornamental elements.

Cover of Farshid Moussavi and Michael Kubo, *The Function of Ornament*, Actar, 2006. From Kazuyo Sejima's Christian Dior Omotesando Store in Tokyo to the Herzog & de Meuron Laban Dance Centre in London, the book offers a comprehensive catalogue of contemporary ornamental practice. It has been used as a practical guide by architecture students around the world.

Poster for one of Adolf Loos's lectures on 'Ornament and Crime' given in 1913 in Vienna. The argument of Loos's famous essay was tested from 1909 on, in a series of lectures given in Berlin and Vienna such as this one.

Ludwig Mies van der Rohe, Barcelona Pavilion, 1929.
In Mies van der Rohe's German pavilion for the Barcelona Universal Exhibition, the precious materials – marble, red onyx and travertine – are not the only ornamental elements. The pieces of furniture designed by the architect, the Barcelona chairs, also appear as ornaments.

In the late work of Le Corbusier, the traces left by the concrete formwork belong to this neo-ornamental vocabulary; they are actually supposed to make the viewer aware of the productive hand of the construction worker in a way that is strongly reminiscent of one of the key functions of ornament according to 19th-century English theorist John Ruskin.[5] The ornamental character of elements like the Modulor Man at the entrance of the Unités d'Habitation of Marseilles (1952) and Firminy (1967) is even more evident.

In *The Function of Ornament*, Farshid Moussavi and Michael Kubo show themselves aware of this ornamental dimension of modern architecture. In addition to contemporary realisations, they review examples like Frank Lloyd Wright's Johnson Wax Laboratory Tower (1950) with its rhythmic use of bands, or Gordon Bunshaft's Beinecke Rare Book Library on Yale Campus (1963) with its sophisticated play on the translucence of marble.[6] They could have added many other cases, like the decorative use of brick by French

Le Corbusier, Unité d'Habitation of Marseilles, 1952.
In true Ruskinian manner, the irregular traces of the formwork on the pilotis contribute to the overall impression of harmony of the construction. At La Chaux-de-Fonds in Switzerland, Le Corbusier had received an initial education permeated by Arts and Crafts ideals. From Marseilles to Chandigarh, the influence of these ideals becomes noticeable in many of his postwar realisations.

architect Roland Simounet at the Lille Museum of Modern Art (1983) recently extended by Manuelle Gautrand.[7]

But one should avoid excessive generalisation when drawing on these examples. Neither the Johnson Wax Laboratory nor the Beinecke Rare Book Library openly claimed an ornamental character. At the time of their completion, ornament was officially supposed to belong to the past, just like architectural styles that Le Corbusier had famously compared to the feathers in a woman's hat in *Toward an Architecture*.[8] Above all, modern ornamental practices remained secondary to the quest for architectural space, a quest that was generally linked to a tectonic approach to construction, as Kenneth Frampton has convincingly argued.[9] Defined as the way structural elements contributed to the production of space, the tectonic proved far more important to the Modernist project than the scattered ornamental elements that had survived Loos's condemnation.

At the turn of the 1970s and '80s, Postmodernism began explicitly to reintroduce the question of ornament. As critic Charles Jencks remarked, with Modernism 'ornament, polychromy, metaphor, humor, symbolism, and convention were put on the index, and all forms of decoration and historical reference were declared taboo'.[10] To overcome what they perceived as a dramatic self-mutilation of the discipline, architects like Leon Krier even

'Caesars Palace signs and statuary', photograph illustrating Robert Venturi, Denise Scott Brown, Steven Izenour, *Learning from Las Vegas: The Forgotten Symbolism of Architectural Form*, 1972.

In Venturi, Scott Brown and Izenour's manifesto, Modernist architecture is criticised for its attempt to substitute tectonic articulation for ornament, and more generally to substitute expressivity for symbolism. With its kitsch mix of billboards and artistic replicas, Las Vegas appears as a possible antidote to this shift.

tried to return to the use of architectural orders. But for the majority of the theorists and practitioners involved in the reaction against the shortcomings of Modernism, ornament remained secondary to the issue of symbolism and semiotics. It epitomised one of the ways in which architecture could reconnect with its various audiences. But it was not the only path, far from it. Ornament was certainly not at the epicentre of the Postmodern enterprise, even if Jencks listed it among the key dimensions banned by Modernism. It played a relatively minor role in the writings of Colin Rowe, Aldo Rossi or Robert Venturi, even though the 'ducks' and other billboard signs invoked by the latter in *Learning from Las Vegas* possessed an ornamental dimension. Typology, composition and their symbolic potential presented far more pressing issues.

The widespread return of ornament that can be observed today is actually inseparable from the massive diffusion of the computer in the architectural

Ruy Klein, Klex 1, installation, New York City, 2008.
This CNC-milled high-density foam finished in pearl-gold Chromalusion offers a striking example of the new possibilities of ornamentation through digital modelling and fabrication. The result possesses a strong organic connotation. It appears simultaneously reminiscent of the intricacies of Islamic and Gothic vaults, not to mention Antonio Gaudi's architecture.

profession that had started by the mid-1990s. Since the early steps taken in this direction like Columbia University's 'Paperless Studio' – founded by Greg Lynn, Hani Rashid and Scott Marble – that clearly marked a turning point, design software and computer-aided fabrication have opened new ornamental perspectives. It is possible to generate textures and patterns with previously unknown ease. Complex geometries have become accessible to anyone who knows how to use a computer. In this regard, 3D printers, laser cutters, mills and routers have simplified the realisation of intricate ornamental elements.[11]

But there are more profound driving forces in the affair than mere instrumental facilitation. As noted elsewhere, the rise of digital culture in architecture has been accompanied by the weakening of the tectonic approach and the increased importance attached to surface.[12] In many contemporary projects, the envelope seems to matter much more than the structure. If Frank Gehry's projects, such as the Guggenheim Museum Bilbao (1997) or the Walt Disney Concert Hall in Los Angeles (2003), offer perhaps the most striking expression of this attitude, similar tendencies can be observed in many other instances.

This evolution is linked to broad technological and programmatic evolutions. With regards to technology, the battlefront has moved towards the periphery of the building with the new energetic and environmental requirements implied by sustainability. The distribution of stresses and strains inside its structural members tends to matter less today than the exchange of heat and light between exterior and interior. The evolution of programs reinforces the strategic character of the envelope that appears

Marc-Antoine Laugier, frontispiece of the second edition of the *Essai sur l'Art*, 1755. According to Laugier, the primitive hut is both the origin of the architectural tectonic and the initial incentive for decoration.

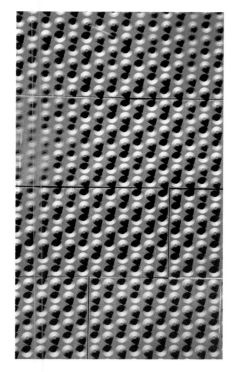

often disconnected from interiors, which should be as flexible as possible to allow for periodic change of destination. One is confronted with a growing number of 'blank' building types, department stores, shopping malls and even museums that do not presuppose an organic relation between the outside and the inside. In this context, 'the architect's role is becoming increasingly specialized in the design of the outer shell, leaving the interior to other designers'.[13]

Could ornament represent a mere antidote to the risk of seeing architecture disappear under the pressure of sustainability or programmatic requirements? After all, this would not be the first time that the discipline would define itself around the notion of a decorated shed. During the second half of the 18th century, in relation to the rise of new utilitarian concerns, theorists like Marc-Antoine Laugier had already suggested such a path. For Laugier, architecture had developed from the archetype of the primitive hut by transposing its tectonic principles into stone and, above all, by adorning it.[14] Should one interpret the contemporary return of ornament in a similar perspective? Despite the superficial analogy, there are profound differences between then and now, between the conception of ornament that prevailed in the 18th century, at the time of Laugier and his primitive hut, and the present-day understanding of the term. Such dissimilarity should make us cautious about the sense of déjà vu that may be experienced now and then when listening to contemporary architectural debate.

Herzog & de Meuron, De Young Museum, San Francisco, 2005.
The envelope of the De Young Museum is based on a complex series of transformations starting with an image of vegetation on the site, which is inverted, then pixellated. In the following stage, the pixels are translated into protruding or depressed dots of varying depths. Finally, a series of perforations for light and ventilation purposes are superimposed on this pattern. The resulting envelope seems to merge view and touch.

Textures, Patterns and Topology: A Different Ornament

Under the influence of digital tools, today's ornament indeed presents a series of new features. First, ornament often lies in the superficial texture, which the computer enables us to modulate and represent on the screen with a vividness that transforms it into an essential part of the design. Of course, texture was always an important aspect of architecture. But digital technology has allowed it to become a more autonomous dimension, present from the start in the design process and imbued with a definite ornamental

Francis Soler, French Ministry of Culture, Paris, 2004.
In Soler's project, the image that serves as a basis for the composition is distorted in a way reminiscent of anamorphosis. The result evokes some gossamer-thin web cast on the building.

character. Moreover, as Stephen Perrella has noted, computer software makes possible the texturing of any surface with any picture, thus blurring the distinction between texture and image.[15] The play with this new continuum has led to ornamental practices ranging from 'pixellation' to extended 'wallpaperisation'. In projects ranging from the San Francisco De Young Museum (2005) to the Minneapolis Walker Art Center (2005), Herzog & de Meuron have made extensive use of pixellation techniques. Francis Soler's silver screen for the French Ministry of Culture in Paris (2004) provides a good example of wallpaperisation. The abstract lace that envelops the buildings is actually the result of a computer-aided deformation of a Renaissance composition by Giulio Romano.

György Kepes, illustrations provided for Norbert Wiener's article, 'Pure Patterns in a Natural World', published in Kepes, *The New Landscape in Art and Science*, 1956.
In the 1950s, patterns related information and the visible world. They play a central role in Kepes's reflections on the connections between science and art. Their ornamental character appeared as the direct result of underlying regularities at work in the physical or social worlds. A few years later, they were mobilised by Christopher Alexander in his *Notes on the Synthesis of Form*, which attempt to rebuild the architectural discipline on new foundations compatible with nascent computer-programming techniques.

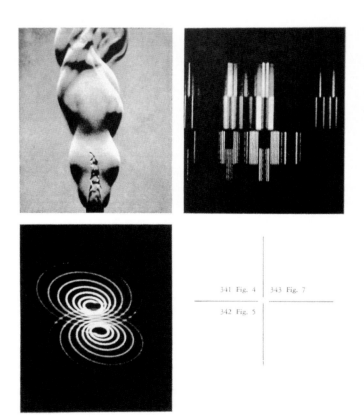

341 Fig. 4   343 Fig. 7

342 Fig. 5

Second, pattern that used to play a relatively minor role in the Western ornamental tradition, contrary to the Islamic one, now appears as one of the most common forms taken by ornament in contemporary projects. Many examples of contemporary architectural ornamentation are based on patterning and related practices such as tessellation. Foreign Office Architects' Spanish Pavilion at the Aichi World Expo of 2005 uses tessellation, for instance. From the 1950s on, patterns have been present in many enterprises that tried to relate computer and cybernetic culture to arts and design. They were, for instance, at the core of György Kepes's attempts to weave together information and the visible organisation of our environment in exhibitions and books like his 1956 *The New Landscape in Art and Science* in which authors like cyberneticist Norbert Wiener are placed side by side with architects like Richard Neutra.[16] In contrast with the limited character of these pioneering experiments, the novelty lies in the generalisation of the use of patterns on building facades today. This diffusion has been facilitated again by computer software. With the possibilities offered to the designer to manage complex patterns through deformation, tiling and tessellation, they constitute one of the bases of contemporary ornamental practices.

NOX, Maison Folie, Lille, France, 2004.
'We made the black box glow with a luminous skin that transforms with movement in and around the *Maison Folie*, a shimmering, almost holographic dress that incorporates the pulsation of art and life', writes Lars Spuybroek on a project where the entire facade becomes ornamental.

Lastly, the very movement of the facade can become ornamental. With their soft curves imbued with an almost Baroque fluidity, Lars Spuybroek's Maison Folie in Lille (2004) or Jeanne Gang's Aqua Tower in Chicago (2010) clearly illustrate this possibility fostered by the ease with which designers can now manipulate complex geometry and 'animate' form, to use Greg Lynn's expression.[17] The twisting movement of the facade of Preston Scott Cohen's Tel Aviv Museum of Art (2011) may also be interpreted in this manner. Like another facade, interior this time, the central 'Lightfall' of the building possesses an even clearer ornamental turn. Beside texture and pattern, topology is part of contemporary ornamental vocabulary.

Beyond these three well-defined possibilities, a whole range of hybrid ornamental practices have also emerged. Although the figure of the continuous fold belongs in principle to the topological category, it has been often reduced to something more graphic, pattern-like, in buildings like Diller, Scofidio + Renfro's Boston Institute of Contemporary Art (2006). In numerous cases, the structural elements tend also to acquire an ornamental character, often in relation to a desire of liberation from an allegedly Cartesian frame.[18] Voronoi tessellations or Weaire-Phelan structures, such as the one used for the Beijing Water Cube (2008) by PTW Architects, are typical of this blurring between the structural and the ornamental. In close proximity to the Water Cube, the confusion between these traditionally distinct genres can also be observed in a building like Herzog & de Meuron's Olympic Stadium (2008), also known as the 'Bird's Nest'. Its net of beams – some load bearing, others not – possesses a surprisingly ornamental turn, which is somewhat detrimental to traditional structural legibility, as if traditional tectonic principles did not matter any more.

With its frequent use of intricate geometric patterns and tessellation, contemporary

Preston Scott Cohen, Tel Aviv Museum of Art, 2011. The central 'Lightfall' of Preston Scott Cohen's Tel Aviv Museum of Art extension appears both as the expression of the overall logic of the building, which was generated through a double movement of stacking and twisting, and as a gratuitous moment of architectural bliss. It may be seen as a giant ornament; just as the entire new building itself can be interpreted as an ornament for the city.

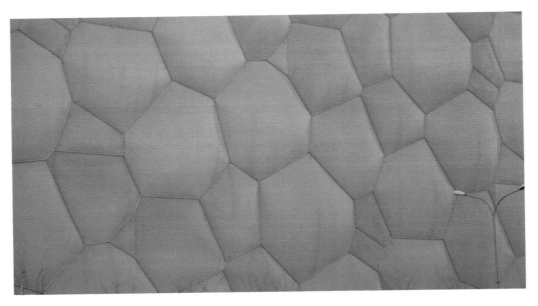

digitally designed ornament is sometimes reminiscent of Islamic décor. Zaha Hadid has explicitly played on this connection, for example, in the Marsa Dubai Residential Tower project (2005). To explore it fully could be in itself the subject of an essay. Here we would prefer to insist on the difference between contemporary ornamentation and a Western tradition of ornament that developed from the Renaissance on, claiming for a long time the theoretical heritage of Roman architect and engineer Vitruvius, as well as a practical inspiration derived from the study of Ancient monuments.[19] This Vitruvian tradition exerted its influence well into the 19th century, and even beyond, if one takes into account some of the aforementioned ornamental practices of modern architecture.

In this book, we will also leave aside the European Middle Ages and their treatment of ornamentation. Romanesque and Gothic will appear only when revived by the age of industry in a perspective that in fact owes a lot to the conception of architecture and architectural décor that had emerged at the Renaissance. Neo-Romanesque and neo-Gothic are not Romanesque and Gothic, but hybrids between medieval formal references, the architectural legacy of Renaissance and Baroque, and 19th-century concerns. Once again, the Vitruvian tradition and its reinterpretation of Greco-Roman architecture represent our true point of departure.

PTW Architects, CSCEC + Design and Arup, Beijing National Aquatics Centre, 2007.
The Weaire-Phelan pattern on which the design of the Water Cube is based derives from the natural formation of bubbles in foam. Under the irregularity of the superficial patterns lies a geometry that can also be found in molecular structures and crystals.

Zaha Hadid, Marsa Dubai Residential Tower, 2005. In this project, the influence of Islamic décor can easily be traced in the overall pattern used for the facades, even if this pattern is less easy to read when wrapped around the tower.

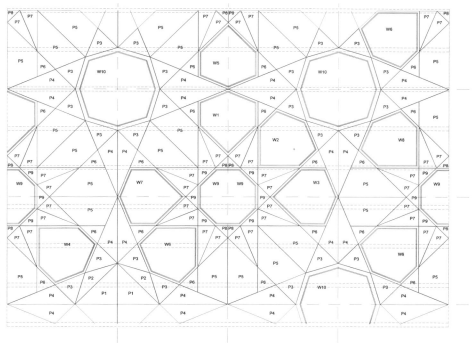

The differences between today's ornament and the conception that prevailed within the frame of the Vitruvian tradition actually go much deeper than the increased importance of textures, patterns and topology. In Renaissance and Baroque architecture, ornament seldom covered the entirety of the buildings' facades and interiors. It was usually concentrated at certain key points. Well into the 19th century, some of these key points were directly correlated with the use of architectural orders. Even when orders did not fulfil a purely aesthetic purpose – when columns were invested with a real load-bearing function for instance – they carried a profusion of ornaments like delicate and complex mouldings, intricately carved capitals, friezes. But even the most ornamented facades had to show some restraint. Overabundance jeopardised one of the fundamental roles of ornament, which was to reinforce the main rhythms of architectural ordinance rather than merely spreading a decorative layer over them. As the 17th-century French painter Nicolas Poussin explained

Basilica of the Holy Cross in Lecce, Italy, completed in 1695.
The upper part of the facade of the church of the Holy Cross in Lecce presents an unusually rich ornamentation with exuberant floral motives, fantastic animals and grotesque figures. The intricate, almost fractal décor seems a curious hybrid between the Vitruvian codes and the highly personal inspiration of architect Giuseppe Zimbalo (1617–1710), the main designer of the facade.

in one of his letters, one had to refrain from 'the confusion of ornaments …
(which) were invented only to soften the severity of simple architecture'.[20]

Every principle has its exceptions. In a number of circumstances, this restraint
was not followed. The upper part of the facade of the Basilica of the Holy
Cross in Lecce, Italy (1695), does not fit into the dominant model. The
decoration of many Latin-American Baroque churches appears even more
exuberant. Their facades look like heavily decorated altarpieces in which not
a single square foot is left without an ornament of one kind or another. In
some of his extreme compositions, such as those which illustrate his 1765
Osservazioni (…) sopra la Lettre de M Mariette (Observations on the Letter
of Mr Mariette), or his 1769 *Diverse Maniere d'Adornare I Cammini ed Ogni
Altra Parte degli Edifizi* (Diverse Manners
of Ornamenting Chimneys and All Other
Parts of Houses), Giovanni Battista Piranesi
also rejected soberness in the name of the
unbounded power of imagination. But such
exceptions did not invalidate the general rule:
rather than a pervasive condition, ornamental
décor was conceived as a discrete series of
embellishments. Their distribution was not
without analogy with the writing of music:
discontinuous notes that were nevertheless
meant to produce a continuous stream of
sensations and affects.

In addition to theoretical reasons rooted in the
Vitruvian belief in the primacy of order and
proportion, or based on the crucial importance
of composition, which began to be substituted
for Renaissance and Baroque order and
proportion towards the end of the 18th
century,[21] there were also practical reasons for
this approach. Often carved by professional
sculptors, ornament was labour-intensive and
costly. Its price contributed to putting a check
on temptations of unbridled use.

The possibility of a crisis of this dominant
model of reasoned thrift loomed when

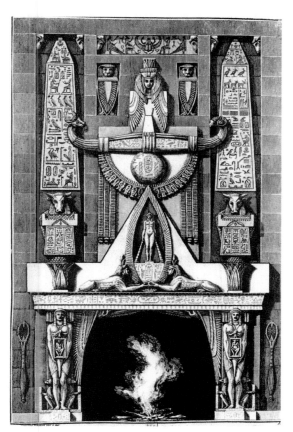

Giovanni Battista Piranesi,
chimney in the Egyptian
style, from *Diverse
Maniere d'Adornare I
Cammini ed Ogni Altra
Parte degli Edifizi*, 1769.
Fragmentation, accumulation
and collage are the key
principles at work in such a
composition. In the eyes of
Piranesi, design is primarily a
matter of invention.

new materials enabled the mass production of decorative elements. New possibilities of repetition and proliferation were afforded by 19th-century terracotta and cast-iron ornaments, epitomised by the profuse décor of many American office buildings. The ornamental excesses of many bourgeois exteriors and interiors reinforced an uneasiness to which we will return later in this chapter. Let us note immediately that such unease appeared directly correlated to psychological flaws of the individuals involved in their creation, from the architect to the client, like the symptom of a civilisational disease that called for drastic curative measures.

Giuliano da Sangallo, *Studi di particolari architettonici e piccolo putto*, Codice Vaticano Barberiniano 4424.
On this page of drawings after the Antique by Giuliano da Sangallo (c 1445–1516), ornaments seem to float freely like the detachable fragments they are supposed to be, at least in theory.

This impending crisis – a crisis that was at the origin of Loos's passionate denunciation of what he perceived as a decorative spree inherited from the 19th century – did not lead, however, to the notion that ornament could become something like a general superficial condition. Yet this is precisely what has occurred with the recent return of ornament. In most cases, as texture, pattern or topology, ornament appears as an overall property of the envelope.

This pervasive presence usually goes hand in hand with another feature: the impossibility of imagining the building envelope without its ornamentation. This inseparability is partly linked to the typology of contemporary ornament; textures, patterns and topology appear an integral part of the building skin. It has also to do with techniques of fabrication. Whether carved, milled or extruded, today's ornaments often appear physically inseparable from their support.

Such inseparability might be considered as a minor point, but it actually represents a profound departure from a long tradition of thinking about ornament as something that could be theoretically, but also in many cases practically, separated from the fabric of the building. For the Romans of the Imperial period, ornament constituted a legal category of items usually affixed to the floors, walls and ceilings, such as precious marbles, statues, vases and lamps that could be removed if necessary, contrary to structural elements, and with greater difficulty than mere furniture.[22]

Simultaneously, traditional ornament was generally seen as a marker of the difference between anonymous construction and architecture as an artistic production. Ornament was key in denoting architecture up to the point that the architectural discipline could almost be defined as the art of adorning an otherwise unexpressive fabric. Vitruvian order and proportion needed ornaments and their coordinated effects in order to become fully visible to the spectator. The characterisation of architecture as the art of decorating buildings, an old notion revived by Laugier in the second half of the 18th century, rested on the strategic character of ornamentation.

This led to what one may call the paradox of traditional ornament, namely that ornament was all the more indispensable in that it was actually added, and that one could imagine a building deprived of it. This paradoxical status possessed a philosophical dimension, which expresses itself in the origins of the word. The Latin word for ornament, *ornamentum*, shares, for instance, a common etymological origin with the verb *ordino*, meaning to organise, to order, as if an ornament, any well-conceived ornament, expressed the underlying order of things.[23] This mysterious kinship between ornament and ordering is confirmed by another pair of words, 'cosmetics' and 'cosmos'. Both derive from the Greek verb *kosmein* meaning to adorn as well as to arrange. Again, what seems at stake is the intimate relationship between superficial, almost gratuitous-looking appearances covering reality like make-up applied to a face, and the deep structures present under their thin veil.

From a philosophical standpoint, ornament was an illustration of the disconcerting capacity of the supplement to become a defining feature of that to which it was added, a situation admirably analysed by Jacques Derrida in texts such as *Of Grammatology*.[24] According to Derrida, the supplement is neither outside nor inside, neither accidental nor essential in the philosophical sense of these terms. It marks a paradoxical threshold, the possibility of an indefinite process of differentiation that is characteristic of Western thought, although philosophy has repeatedly tried to establish a clear hierarchy between the non-structural and the structural, the accidental and the essential. Through its capacity to be both added and indispensable, ornament challenged such hierarchy. Actually, the attitude of architects towards ornament balanced between two opposite approaches that epitomised this disturbing mode of existence. On the one hand, they had to recognise that ornament was not strictly speaking structural. On the other hand, they were tempted to define it in intimate connection with the fundamental articulations of the building, with its overall structure and proportions. Despite the conception of ornament as lavish décor that had begun to prevail in Imperial Rome, Vitruvius himself had tried to enforce this restrictive definition.[25] As we will see in the next chapter, the crucial questions of licence and invention were inseparable from the problems raised by the ambiguity of ornament.

Because it blurred the distinction between the non-structural and the structural, the status of supplement implied also that ornament did not correspond to an entirely stable category of objects. In other words, something could be both ornamental at a certain level and structural at another. Such was the case of the column that was sometimes presented as the most important ornament of architecture, sometimes as its fundamental structural element. This ambivalence was already present in Alberti for whom the column was both a 'strengthened part of the wall' and an ornament, an ambivalence duly noted by Rudolf Wittkower in *Architectural Principles in the Age of Humanism* who spoke of Alberti's 'incongruous statements on columns'.[26] It explained why, from Alberti to Semper, architectural theorists almost never approached ornament as a fixed collection of parts and elements, but rather as the result of a series of operations of differentiation between supported fixtures and their supports. Many parts and elements in a building could appear alternatively as supported and supporting.

Just as traditional ornament supplemented the fabric of buildings, architecture itself was for a long time interpreted as a supplement of construction. Hence the fascination and disturbance it was met with by philosophy, if we are there again to follow Derrida.[27] On the one hand, architecture seemed to possess a clear foundational character; on the other hand, this foundational character was threatened by its supplementary status. Architectural expression began to unfold at the point when the structural was no longer the only dimension present. Returning to the mythic apologue of the primitive hut, it is worth noting that this process began precisely at the point when the wood structure was translated into stone, a process that deprived some elements of their original constructive function, thus giving birth to the tension between the structural and the ornamental and to the possibility of an autonomous aesthetic expression. For Vitruvius, this process of translation was the true foundation of ornament. In his *Histoire de l'Architecture* (History of Architecture), published in 1899, engineer and architect Auguste Choisy would give the definitive interpretation of the Doric style as a derivative from carpentry.[28]

The conception of architectural ornament as a necessary supplement remained present throughout the 19th century, in the writings of theorists such as Gottfried Semper as well as in the works of architects such as

Auguste Choisy, the origin of Doric ornaments, from *Histoire de l'Architecture*, 1899.
In his monumental history of architecture, Choisy gives the definitive interpretation of how key elements of Doric décor such as triglyphs, metopes, mutules and guttas may be interpreted as direct transposition of carpentry assemblages into stone.

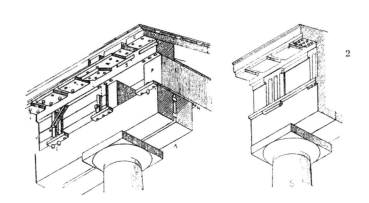

2

Karl Friedrich Schinkel, facade and terracotta panels décor of the Bauakademie in Berlin, 1836, from *Sammlung architektonischer Entwürfe*, 1858.
The Bauakademie offers a brilliant demonstration of how ornament can be both added and essential. The terracotta panels were meant to evoke the origins and early developments of construction and architecture in Greece and Rome, their subsequent fall, their new rise in the Middle Ages, from the ruins of Antiquity, and their final triumph in the age of reason and industry.

Karl Friedrich Schinkel or Louis Sullivan. 'One must not understand the word ornamentation or decoration to indicate something that lies outside the object and its essence or essential idea,' declared Schinkel.[29] At Schinkel's Bauakademie (1836), the terracotta ornamental panels appeared both conspicuously added to the structure of the building and absolutely essential to the composition. They reinforced its structural articulations while commenting on its function – to house a school of architecture – by providing a reflection on the origin and development of the architectural discipline. The role of ornament was equally determining in Sullivan's Wainwright Building in St Louis (1891) where its rhythm was an integral part of the overall tectonic expression.

Until the dawn of the 20th century, ornament remained in the eyes of many architects an essential supplement to the tectonic. Modern architecture ruined this conception by relegating it to the status

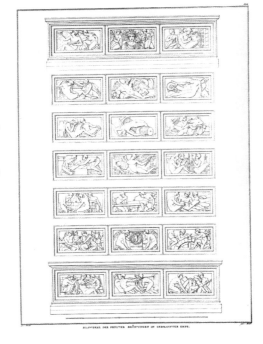

Louis Sullivan, Wainwright Building in Saint Louis, 1891.
The Wainwright ranks among the most accomplished solutions given by Sullivan to the problem of the skyscraper. Ornaments are added and at the same time constitutive of the overall organisation of the facade. The contrast between the ornamented spandrels and the bare vertical piers reinforces the latter. Interestingly, one pier out of two does not encase a steel support. Décor appears both as a lie and as the revelation of the higher truth of the steel frame, that of a rhythmic dynamism.

of mere accessory – Le Corbusier's feathers in the hat – even if its remnants did not always conform to this demeaning attitude in practice.

Although ornament has regained importance in contemporary design, it has certainly not recovered this supplementary status, far from it. As a pervasive condition, it appears inseparable from the envelope. Thus, it is impossible to consider it both as added and essential. This major difference with the past should in itself represent an incentive to question the notion of a mere

return of what was. There is as much invention as recovery in the affair, the invention of a new type of ornamentation fundamentally different from the traditional one.

Such difference accounts for another puzzling feature of contemporary architectural production: the capacity of what used to be considered as pure structure to appear ornamental. The Beijing 2008 Olympic Stadium designed by Herzog & de Meuron, the so-called 'Bird's Nest', provides a good example of this transgression of established boundaries. In an interview with French art historian and critic Jean-François Chevrier, Jacques Herzog insists on the blurring between structure and ornament that characterises such a project.[30] Its crisscross of beams evokes some giant piece of jewellery, especially at the end of a beautiful day, when the setting sun gives it a golden hue, or at night when the network of beams becomes more transparent.

The current situation is not entirely comparable to the ambiguity that used to prevail in some cases between the structural and the ornamental, in as far as in many cases it now affects elements that were not supposed to possess a potentially ornamental character. It is as if ornament were contaminating structure instead of playing the complex game of supplementarity with it.

Herzog & de Meuron, Olympic Stadium, Beijing, 2008.
One of the objectives of the architects was to avoid creating a mere decorative skin. The complex structure generates an intermediary space between outside and inside, city and sports arena. The traditional distinction between the structural and the ornamental no longer applies to an object that tries to transcend these categories.

Manolo Nuñez-Yanowsky, police station of Paris 12th arrondissement, 80 boulevard Daumesnil, 1991.
Michelangelo's *Dying Slave* can be found today in the Louvre. Manolo Nuñez's provocative quotation of this well-known piece of sculpture raises the question of how far you can go in the use of a symbolic architectural décor. Today's refusal of meaning is a direct result of the rejection of such excesses.

Another major difference between traditional and contemporary ornament lies in the systematic refusal of any kind of symbolic meaning, at least publicly. Theorists and practitioners have been almost unanimous on that point. In their *Atlas of Novel Tectonics*, Jesse Reiser and Nanako Umemoto call, for instance, for the use of 'asignifying signs', since 'an architecture that has to explain itself, or be explained, has failed to present its own qualities'.[31] Behind their attitude, one detects the fear of a potential return to some of Postmodernism's most blatant limits: the use of a symbolic vocabulary distributed on the facade of the building without true connection to its overall architectural organisation. With its concrete copies of Michelangelo's *Dying Slave* protruding on its top floor, a police station designed by architect Manolo Nuñez-Yanowsky in Paris (1991) epitomises the extravagant results to which this attitude can lead. In such extreme projects, ornament is definitely heavier than the feather evoked by Le Corbusier, but it is certainly no less gratuitous. Moussavi and Kubo's decision to attribute a 'function' to ornament must be understood in this perspective. Without a function, they believe, ornament would be a mere addition referring itself to a sphere of significations exterior to architecture.

There is an additional factor contributing to the demise of the logic of supplementarity at stake here. For the refusal of any reference that would involve elements located outside the realm of architecture proper, that is architecture understood as a manipulation of spatial and constructive elements, also owes something to the legacy of the 'autonomy project' of the architecture of the 1960s and '70s. From Aldo Rossi and Peter Eisenman to John Hejduk and Bernard Tschumi, the ambition of the architects involved in this project was to construct architecture as a system of knowledge based, there again, on its internal resources rather than on external references borrowed from other fields. As theorist K Michael Hays has argued, this approach led to the production of effects and above all affects, the power of which is currently explored by architects, especially in relation to the use of digital tools.[32]

The current architectural discourse on the importance of affects is rooted in Gilles Deleuze's philosophy and its attempt to shift attention from the traditional interest taken in rhetoric and semiotics to the physical dimension of the artistic experience.[33] In our last chapter, we will return to what this shift implies concretely for architecture. Let us insist for now on the importance of the break with a Western ornamental tradition that possessed a strong figurative and symbolic dimension. The story would, of course, be different if one were to consider the abstract patterns of Islamic ornament.

Greco-Roman architecture already used figurative elements such as plant arabesques, fruit festoons, bucrania, trophies and statues. Renaissance and Baroque architecture continued with a practice that was all the more inseparable from symbolic content in that the orders themselves were imparted with content. After all, the Doric order was supposed to possess

Panel from the Ara Pacis Augustae, Altar of Augustan Peace, Rome, 9 BC.
The lower part of the décor of the Ara Pacis Augustae comprises a frieze with scrolling acanthus tendrils, a vivid evocation of nature's fertility.

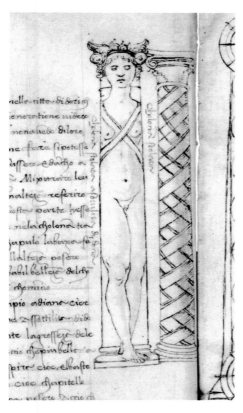

Francesco di Giorgio, Ionic column, after Codice Ashburnham, 361, Biblioteca Medicea Laurenziana, Florence. Italian Renaissance engineer and architect Francesco di Giorgio gives a striking illustration of the traditional analogy between the Classical orders and the male, female and adolescent bodies. Whereas the Doric order is supposed to possess a male character, the Ionic is usually associated with the 'more graceful' female proportions.

a male character, while the Ionic and Corinthian orders were associated respectively with the female and maiden characters. Many ornaments referred themselves to the reign of nature or to the world of human society and culture. Architectural décor often mixed the two to suggest the passage from one to another. During the last decades of the 18th century, such passage would become a favourite theme of architects such as Etienne-Louis Boullée and Claude-Nicolas Ledoux. Beyond the immediate allusion to the function of his saltworks of Arc-et-Senans (1779), Ledoux's ornamental motive of horizontal vases protruding from the wall, from which water petrified by salt hangs like ice on the edge of a roof, conveys this very notion of the transition from nature to civilisation, from rock salt and brines as a natural resource to the realisation of its use for humans. This ornamental motive echoes the statement made at the gate of the saltworks through the contrast between irregular blocks of stone symbolising raw nature and the regular columns of the portico that refer to the sophistication of an enlightened century.

The philosophical theme of the transition from nature to civilisation remained present throughout the 19th century, through the frequent juxtaposition of plants, animals and products of human industry. For instance, on the portal of the architecture school accommodated in Schinkel's Bauakademie, the two vertical series of panels evoking the invention of the architectural orders begin by the representation of blooming plants in order to suggest that human arts may appear as an extension of the spontaneous fecundity of nature. The panels with geniuses rising from plants that decorate the arch of the same portal reinforce this idea.

Somewhere between the immediate representation of natural or artificial objects and general philosophical statements like those made by Ledoux or Schinkel, ornaments could also function at an allegorical level. As such, they conveyed messages often permeated by ideology, from the importance of the arts and sciences for the advancement of civilisation to the benevolent nature of a given political regime or religion. The 19th century proved especially fond of allegories and tended to make excessive use of them, at least according to our taste, which is still, in that respect, influenced by the Modernist condemnation of ornamental abuse. Despite French sculptor Jean-Baptiste Carpeaux's talent (he is the author of the bombastic group called *The Dance* that adorns the facade of the Opéra Garnier), it is difficult not to feel a little perplexed in front of his *Imperial France Bringing Light to the World and Protecting Agriculture and Science* that he designed for the Flore Pavilion of the New Louvre of Napoleon III in the 1860s.

Ledoux, saltworks of Arc-et-Senans, 1779.
The vases that adorn the walls of Claude-Nicolas Ledoux's saltworks of Arc-et-Senans in the east of France are typical of the ambition of late-18th-century architecture to 'speak' through its general disposition as well as through highly symbolic ornaments.

Many 19th-century theorists and practitioners already felt this kind of unease in front of the proliferation of allegories outside and inside the buildings of their time. Their unease stemmed from an impression of imbalance between the visual pleasure that ornament was supposed to arouse and its strong ideological load. Whereas general philosophical statements, or rather suggestions, like the continuity between nature's spontaneous fecundity and man's artistic inspiration were conveyed in such a manner that they did not interfere immediately with visual perception and pleasure, the allegorical message often disrupted it. Above all, it transformed the tension between architectural order and ornament into a highly problematic divorce. If ornament became a 'crime' at the end of the century, it is also because of the way it had been enrolled in the various ideologies of the time.

Until the end of the 19th century, the connection between ornament and questions of meaning and symbols also expressed itself through the intimate relation ornament had with writing. From the Greco-Roman times on, inscriptions had been generally considered as a type of ornament.[34] Baroque Rome was full of inscriptions such as the dedication to Pope Urban VIII Barberini, which adorned the clam-like structure of Gian Lorenzo Bernini's

Jean-Baptiste Carpeaux, plaster model of *Imperial France Bringing Light to the World and Protecting Agriculture and Science*, 1863.
This model of the sculpture that adorns the Louvre's Flore Pavilion offers a good example of the almost immoderate taste of 19th-century official architecture for symbols and allegories. Imperial France is in the centre of the composition seated on an eagle. On the right, Agriculture leaning against a bull; on the left, Science, measuring the earth with a pair of compasses.

Fountain of the Bees (1644). Writing retained an ornamental character until the dawn of modernity as renowned examples such as Labrouste's Bibliothèque Sainte-Geneviève (1851) or McKim, Mead & White's Boston Public Library (1895) make clear. On the facades of both libraries, the lists of great philosophers, writers and artists are part of the décor, just like the friezes, medallions and garlands that contribute to their animation. Despite a few exceptions, inscriptions were included in the Modernist ban on anything that could even remotely be considered as supplementary to architecture.

The Subjective and the Political

If what we call ornament today differs so profoundly from what the term used to mean until the end of the 19th century, why then use the same word and above all speak of a return? It would perhaps be more accurate to evoke the rediscovery of a long-repressed ornamental trend based on different premises than Vitruvian décor.

Despite the gap between traditional and contemporary forms of ornamentation, this essay will explore two intertwined threads that link them and actually constitute a sufficient motive to cling to the notion of return. The first of these threads is the subjective dimension: incorporating both the expression of the architect/designer and the perceptions or responses of the viewer/user. From the Renaissance on, architectural ornament possessed a strongly subjective dimension. First, it was supposed to say something about the artist that had conceived it. Theoretically, this artist was the architect himself, although in many cases sculptors or painters intervened in its conception and realisation. The possibility and even need for personal expression often conflicted with the respect of rules, hence the recurring debates on the extent of the permissible 'licences' that artists could take in order to convey the singularity of their inspiration.

Sculpted, carved, moulded or painted, ornament was generally realised by specialised craftsmen who also left their mark in the process. This mark did not really interest Vitruvian theory, which concentrated mainly on how to limit it to ensure that the architect's intentions were carried into effect with the utmost possible faithfulness. With the possibility to mass-produce ornament with machines and the impersonal character it conferred upon ornament, the trace of the hand began to appear in a more positive light. Ruskin based his entire theory of ornamentation on this trace in which he saw the precondition for imparting matter with true spiritual content.

Finally, ornament was meant to be seen and appreciated. It was also supposed to say something about the social rank and personal achievements of the client who had ordered its realisation. There again, tensions periodically arose between the coercive rules of the art of architecture and individual aspirations. Towards the end of the 18th century, to the dismay of guardians of the Vitruvian tradition such as French theorist Jacques-François Blondel, the power of rules began to wane under the pressure of these individual aspirations. The time was ripe for all kinds of experiments regarding the possibility for owners to see their subjectivity mirrored in the architectural décor that they had chosen for themselves. Nouveau-riche ostentation and bourgeois bad taste became possible, thus paving the way for Loos's condemnation of all that was untamed and vulgar in the abuse of ornamentation.

These various themes and questions will be reviewed in more detail in the next chapter. They all relate to the importance of the subjective dimension throughout the history of Western ornamental theories and practices. It is worth noting that Loos's condemnation of ornament as crime based itself on this subjective character. For the Viennese architect, ornament represented a crime in that it contradicted the essential values of modern individuality. Today, ornament relates again to the question of the subject, although in a way that differs from the past. Part of the difference comes from a new understanding of the relation between buildings and their viewers, a relation interpreted as an affective continuum instead of being founded on distant appreciation. In the last chapter of this book, the full extent of this shift in connection to the rise of digital culture and its various implications for the architectural discipline will be discussed.Politics, or rather the political relevance of ornament, constitutes another possible thread linking past and present. Although this dimension appears at first less evident than the subjective one, it used to be present on three grounds at least. First, ornament was generally associated with capital and labour expense. Thus, ornament had to do with ostentatious wealth and power. The Roman Empire had perfectly understood this function of ornament. Rome and the major cities of the Empire were adorned with rare marbles and precious statues, which expressed the strength of the regime through its capacity to spend lavishly. The Roman Catholic Church, which claimed part of its heritage, emulated this taste for magnificence. In both cases, ornament was enrolled in a project of domination. From Louis XIV's Versailles and its various copies in late 17th- and 18th-century Europe, to the Soviet attempt to create an architectural décor celebrating the triumph of the masses and its American counterpart that shaped places like Washington, many other politics of ornament can be identified throughout history.

This first function of ornament as a display of political power reveals itself inseparable from a second role as a medium carrying politically significant messages. Until the end of the 19th century, as we have seen, ornament conveyed philosophical and ideological notions. Above all, it constituted an indicator of the relative importance of the institutions and people associated with the construction of a building. Traditional ornament was as much hierarchical as symbolic. Whereas numerous studies have been devoted to its symbolic content, its role as an index of social rank has been less thoroughly investigated.

Last but not least, ornament was also instrumental in the quest for an immersive decorative order that possessed a strong political character. In the eyes of Renaissance and Baroque theorists and practitioners of architecture, ornament was part of the process that transformed inhospitable settings into habitations for mankind. This contribution proved especially crucial in cities that were, almost by definition, adorned places.

The lesson of Imperial Rome had never been forgotten. Through their repetition and modulation, architectural ornaments were constitutive of this place-making that was in essence political.

The third chapter of this book will evoke more precisely the political dimension of traditional ornament. Now, contrary to subjectivity, the political has not yet fully returned with contemporary architectural ornamentation, if only because of the refusal to deal frontally with meaning and symbols, a refusal all the more paradoxical that the accent is put simultaneously on the role of architecture as a medium. How can architecture be a medium without carrying any clear message? This does not prevent the political dimension from haunting today's ornamental practice through concerns ranging from the quest for a certain degree of lavishness to the desire to create immersive environments, which goes hand in hand with the accent placed on affect. Politics is also very much present in the debates regarding sustainability. Is this enough? As argued in the final chapter, a true politics of ornament might actually require us to re-engage with architectural meaning. How can this be done without falling again into the Postmodern traps of pastiche and collage? The task is among the most daunting that await contemporary designers.

In the history of Western ornament, until the end of the 19th century, subjectivity and politics had been connected through a triadic structure: pleasure and beauty, social rank and prestige, communication and knowledge. With regards to ornament, these three concerns functioned in a manner strangely reminiscent of how the famous Vitruvian triad – beauty, commodity and solidity – defined the object of architecture. They corresponded to the most fundamental purposes of ornamentation. Simultaneously, they bridged the gap between the individual and the collective, thus contributing to the articulation of the subjective and the political.

The quest for pleasure and beauty constituted one of the fundamental roles of ornament in the Vitruvian tradition. Ornament emphasised but also softened and made more vibrant the overall composition. The pleasure derived from its perception was both experienced at an individual level and invested with civic value. With the exception of Sparta, it was the ambition of every Greek city to adorn the public monuments of its acropolis. One should not underestimate this collective relevance. Ornament appeared as a fundamental component of a shared sense of aesthetic. As Oleg Grabar has argued, the manner in which a society approaches the question of adornment and derives pleasure from it, from clothing to buildings, is

Gian Lorenzo Bernini,
Fountain of the Bees,
Rome, 1644.
The papal city remained
faithful to Ancient Rome's
use of inscriptions as
ornaments. The fountain
designed by Bernini is
dedicated to Pope Urban VIII
Barberini. The bees situated
on the bottom of the clam,
which give their name to the
monument, were the symbol
of the Barberini family.

inseparable from the way it relates more generally to its visible environment,
to the world of objects and forms.[35] This relation is in its turn inseparable
from the way its conceives the place of man on the earth, between the realm
of nature and the kingdom of the gods.

Rank and prestige appeared as another common concern when using
architectural ornaments, since décor was supposed to say something about
the social condition of the patron of the adorned building. But this function
extended there again beyond individual identity for it referred as much to the
overall hierarchical organisation of society as to the position occupied by a
given person in that hierarchy. As an indicator of social status, ornament was
part of a system of social distinction, to use Bourdieu's concept,[36] a role well
conveyed by the term 'decorum' that designates both the dignity appropriate

Henri Labrouste, Sainte Geneviève library in Paris, 1851.
The facade of Labrouste's celebrated library bears the names of 810 religious leaders, literary authors, philosophers and scientists, from Moses to 19th-century Swedish chemist Jöns Jacob Berzelius. With these lists, the building becomes analogous to the books it houses.

to a specific occasion or function and the way artistic expression may serve this purpose. Until the end of the 19th century, ornament was very much about decorum, even if it regularly challenged social conventions. It lost this role with modernity. Modern architecture proved perhaps more revolutionary in its rejection of any form of association between décor and social hierarchy than in the severe restrictions it brought to the use of ornaments. The difficulty that it experienced in defining new codes of monumentality was directly related to this drastic departure from what had been one of the most enduring features of Western architecture since the Renaissance.

In many situations, architectural ornament also related to the pursuit of communication and knowledge and to the old ideal of a building that would offer easily accessible lessons to individuals as well as to society as a whole through its tectonic organisation and décor. In this perspective, ornament was supposed to possess a pedagogical value directly linked to its meaning. This relation to knowledge is perhaps a specificity of architectural ornament. Eighteenth-century 'architecture parlante', speaking architecture, marked the climax of the belief in the pedagogical value of public monuments.[37] Many ornaments used by Boullée and Ledoux conveyed moral lessons to the viewer. The vases protruding from the walls of the Arc-et-Senans saltworks were one instance of them.

Despite Victor Hugo's famous statement in Notre-Dame de Paris that 'ceci tuera cela', that writing and printing had replaced public buildings, cathedrals in particular, as the privileged instrument of collective memory and instruction, 19th-century architects still believed that their discipline had a special relation to knowledge, and ornamentation contributed to its expression.[38] In Labrouste and McKim, Mead & White's, but also Pugin and Jones's compositions, the pedagogical dimension of ornamentation represented a further motive to integrate inscriptions in architectural décor.[39] The connection between ornamentation and knowledge was there again lost with Modernism, which preferred to concentrate on the expressive potential of the tectonic.

Pleasure and beauty, rank and prestige, communication and knowledge: this triadic structure has not yet fully returned with contemporary architecture, and this incompleteness may allow us to understand better what remains to be achieved to foster the re-emergence of a true politics of ornament. Pleasure is back for sure, even if beauty remains a somewhat unclear issue. In many cases, the ugly appears as the new form taken by beauty; for some of his projects, Hernan Diaz Alonzo goes as far as to claim the grotesque and the horrific as relevant aesthetic categories.[40] In addition to pleasure, social ranking and prestige have also begun to reappear. From cultural programmes to high-end retail shops and restaurants, the use of ornament is often related to a renewed quest for distinction. Still missing are, of course, the gradations that led to more modest programmes, but their return is not impossible to imagine. Intelligible content related to knowledge remains, however, utterly absent. Contemporary ornament has not yet been willing or able to reconnect with the cognitive dimension of the ornamental tradition, as if affective experience were incompatible with knowledge. Are we destined to float in a state of bliss in the new sensorium designed for us like goldfish in a bowl? Architectural ornament was not only meant to arouse pleasure; it was supposed to stimulate the reflexive faculties of the spectator. One of the most common ways it achieved this goal was through the confrontation between tradition and novelty, rules and exception. Ornament was connected to enduring visual codes that were interpreted in a singular manner, thus provoking, at least in certain situations, a mix of recognition and surprise. Beyond mere delight, this mix introduced the spectator to one of the most fundamental dimensions of architecture: that of a reflection on time, past, present and future, and on the fate of human institutions. Codes have been lost and rules remain uncertain. By the same token, we tend to live in an overextended present, oblivious to the past and impervious to the demands of a future that would look truly different from what lies before our eyes.

In the end, why should we be concerned by the return of ornament? The answer is twofold. Ornament represents an intriguing phenomenon for theorists, critics and historians. As such it deserves their attention and needs to be accounted for. But it constitutes above all an opportunity for contemporary architecture to overcome some of its shortcomings and avoid serious pitfalls. The ornamental dimension is all the more important today in that it coexists with the renewed desire to interpret architecture in the mere light of usefulness, as a tool providing infrastructural support for sustainable life. To the reader of Manfredo Tafuri, this desire to be useful strangely echoes the Modernist ambition to transform architecture into the very instrument of political, economic and social rationalisation. In *Architecture and Utopia*, the preeminent Italian historian denounced the illusory character of such an ambition.[41] We may be confronted sometimes with a similar illusion when we are told that architecture's mission is to save the world, now that engineering has shown its limits as a potential saviour.

The suggestion here is not that the architectural discipline should remain indifferent to the pressing issues of the time, far from it. But its way to address them shouldn't be detrimental to its core values like the quest for the pleasurable, and yes, let us make use of the word, beauty. Ornament has always had to do with pleasure and beauty. It is also related to the pursuit of a certain type of knowledge in which visual pleasure leads to a reflection on the resources that make architecture expressive. For architects especially, ornament represents a means to reconnect with the reflexive dimension of their discipline. After all, architecture has always been based on a reasoned examination of itself.

This reflexive stance could very well constitute the precondition for the architectural discipline to engage in a truly productive manner with the major challenges of its time – like sustainability – without trying to emulate engineering or planning. It may be worth remembering in passing that 19th-century architecture, with all its ornaments that made it different from engineering, was actually much more efficient in its negotiation with technology than modern architecture. Contrary to what Sigfried Giedion tried to make us believe, architectural modernity was never able easily to enter into dialogue with engineering because of architecture's attempt to subsume it.

To this day, architecture has remained distinct from engineering and more generally from construction, like an irreducible supplement. What if the best way to think about this uncanny situation were to imagine it as a form of ornament?

References

1 Greg Lynn, 'The Structure of Ornament', in Neil Leach, David Turnbull, Chris Williams (eds), *Digital Tectonics* (Chichester, West Sussex: Wiley-Academy, 2004), pp 62–8; Robert Levit, 'Contemporary "Ornament": The Return of the Symbolic Repressed', *Harvard Design Magazine*, no 28, spring/summer 2008, pp 70–85.
2 Farshid Moussavi and Michael Kubo, *The Function of Ornament* (Barcelona: Actar, 2006); Andrea Gleiniger and Georg Vrachliotis, *Pattern: Ornament, Structure, and Behavior* (Basel: Birkhäuser, 2009). See also Mark Garcia (ed), *Patterns of Architecture*, Architectural Design (AD) series (London: John Wiley & Sons, November/December (no 6), 2009.
3 Adolf Loos, 'Ornament and Crime', 1929, republished in Adolf Loos, *Ornament and Crime: Selected Essays* (Riverside, California, Ariadne Press, 1998), pp 167–76, p 167 in particular. On the circumstances surrounding the elaboration of 'Ornament and Crime', see Christopher Long, 'The Origins and Context of Adolf Loos's "Ornament and Crime"', *Journal of the Society of Architectural Historians*, vol 68, no 2, June 2009, pp 200–23.
4 Loos, *Ornament and Crime*, p 171.
5 On the status of formwork in the late Le Corbusier, see, for instance, Sergio Ferro, Chérif Kebbal, Philippe Potié, Cyrille Simonnet, *Le Corbusier: Le Couvent de la Tourette* (Marseilles: Parenthèses, 1988); Roberto Gargiani, Anna Rosellini, *Le Corbusier: Béton Brut and Ineffable Space (1940–1965): Surface Materials and Psychophysiology of Vision* (New York: Routledge, 2011).
6 Moussavi and Kubo, *The Function of Ornament*, pp 28–31, 92–5.
7 See Virginie Picon-Lefebvre, 'Entretien avec Roland Simounet', in Richard Klein (ed) *Roland Simounet à l'œuvre: Architecture 1951–1996* (Villeneuve d'Ascq, Paris: Musée d'Art Moderne Lille Métropole, Institut Français d'Architecture, 2000), pp 35–46.
8 Le Corbusier, *Toward an Architecture* (Paris, 1923, English trs, Los Angeles: Getty Research Institute, 2007), p 101.
9 Kenneth Frampton, *Studies in Tectonic Culture: The Poetics of Construction in Nineteenth and Twentieth Century Architecture* (Cambridge, MA: MIT Press, 1995).
10 Charles Jencks, 'Postmodern and Late Modern: The Essential Definitions', *Chicago Review*, vol 35, no 4, 1987, pp 31–58, p 45 in particular.
11 Cf Antoine Picon, *Digital Culture in Architecture: An Introduction for the Design Professions* (Basel: Birkhäuser, 2010); Mario Carpo, *The Alphabet and the Algorithm* (Cambridge, MA: MIT Press, 2011).
12 Picon, *Digital Culture in Architecture*.
13 Moussavi and Kubo, *The Function of Ornament*, p 5.
14 A new interpretation of Laugier's hut has been proposed by Neil Levine in *Modern Architecture: Representation and Reality* (New Haven, London: Yale University Press, 2009), pp 45–74.
15 Stephen Perrella, 'Electronic

Baroque, Hypersurface II: Autopoiesis', *Hypersurface Architecture II*, Architectural Design, (AD) series (London: John Wiley & Sons), November (no 9–10), 1999, pp 5–7.
16 Reinhold Martin, *The Organizational Complex: Architecture, Media, and Corporate Space* (Cambridge, MA: MIT Press, 2003), pp 38–40 in particular.
17 Greg Lynn, *Animate Form* (New York: Princeton Architectural Press, 1999).
18 See on this theme Cecil Balmond, *Informal* (Munich: Prestel, 2002).
19 On the Vitruvian tradition see, for instance, Hanno-Walter Kruft, *Geschichte der Architekturtheorie* (Munich: CH Beck, 1986); Georg Germann, *Vitruve et le Vitruvianisme: Introduction à l'Histoire de la Théorie Architecturale* (Darmstadt, 1987, French trs, Lausanne: Presses Polytechniques et Universitaires Romandes, 1991); Werner Szambien, *Symétrie Goût Caractère: Théorie et Terminologie de l'Architecture à l'Âge Classique 1500–1800* (Paris: Picard, 1986).

20 Nicolas Poussin, *Lettres de Poussin*, edited by Pierre du Colombier (Paris: A la Cité du Livre, 1929), p 19, quoted by Erika Naginski, 'The Necessity to Embrace', *Thresholds*, no 28, 2005, Essays in Honor of Henry A Millon, p 7.
21 On the notion of composition, see Antoine Picon, 'From Poetry of Art to Method: The Theory of Jean-Nicolas-Louis Durand', introduction to Jean-Nicolas-Louis Durand, *Précis of the Lectures on Architecture with Graphic Portion of the Lectures on Architecture* (Los Angeles: Getty Research Institute, 2000), pp 1–68.
22 Patricia Falguières, 'L'Ornement du Droit', presentation given on 7 November 2011 at the conference *Questionner l'Ornement*, organised by Les Arts Décoratifs and the Institut National d'Histoire de l'Art in Paris, 7–8 November 2011.
23 Pierre Gros, 'La Notion d'Ornamentum de Vitruve à Alberti', *Perspective: La Revue de l'INHA*, 2010–11, 1, pp 130–6, pp 130–1 in particular.
24 Jacques Derrida, *Of*

Grammatology (Paris, 1967, English trs, Baltimore: John Hopkins University Press, 1976).
25 Gros, 'La Notion d'Ornamentum de Vitruve à Alberti', pp 131–2.
26 Rudolf Wittkower, *Architectural Principles in the Age of Humanism* (London, 1949, reprint New York, London: WW Norton, 1971), pp 34–5.
27 Cf Mark Wigley, *The Architecture of Deconstruction: Derrida's Haunt* (Cambridge, MA: MIT Press, 1993).
28 Auguste Choisy, *Histoire de l'Architecture* (Paris: Gauthier-Villars, 1899), pp 225–31. On Choisy's theory, see Thierry Mandoul, *Entre Raison et Utopie: L'Histoire de l'Architecture d'Auguste Choisy* (Wavre, Belgium: Mardaga, 2008).
29 Quoted by Barry Bergdoll, *Karl Friedrich Schinkel: An Architecture for Prussia* (New York: Rizzoli, 1994), p 205.
30 Jean-François Chevrier, Jacques Herzog, 'Ornement, Structure, Espace: Entretien avec Jacques Herzog', in Jean-

François Chevrier, *La Trame et le Hasard* (Paris: L'Arachnéen, 2010), pp 86–109.

31 Jesse Reiser, Nanako Umemoto, *Atlas of Novel Tectonics* (New York: Princeton Architectural Press, 2006), pp 172–3.

32 K Michael Hays, *Architecture's Desire: Reading the Late Avant-Garde* (Cambridge, MA: MIT Press, 2010).

33 See, for instance, Gilles Deleuze, Félix Guattari, *A Thousand Plateaus: Capitalism and Schizophrenia* (Paris, 1980, English trs, Minneapolis: University of Minnesota, 1987).

34 Cf Béatrice Fraenkel, 'Ecriture, Architecture et Ornament: Les Déplacements d'une Problématique Traditionnelle', *Perspective: La Revue de l'INHA,* 2010–11, 1, pp 165–70.

35 Oleg Grabar, *The Mediation of Ornament* (Princeton: Princeton University Press, 1992).

36 Pierre Bourdieu, *Distinction: A Social Critique of the Judgement of Taste* (Paris, 1979, English trs, London: Routledge & Kegan Paul, 1984).

37 Cf Anthony Vidler, *The Writing of the Walls: Architectural Theory in the Late Enlightenment* (New York: Princeton Architectural Press, 1987).

38 Victor Hugo, *Notre-Dame de Paris* (Paris, 1831, reprint Paris: Le Livre de Poche, 1998), p 289.

39 Carol A Hrvol Flores, 'Engaging the Mind's Eye: The Use of Inscriptions in the Architecture of Owen Jones and AWN Pugin', *Journal of the Society of Architectural Historians*, vol 60, no 2, June 2011, pp 158–79.

40 Yael Reisner, Fleur Watson, *Architecture and Beauty* (Chichester, West Sussex: Wiley, 2010), p 255.

41 Manfredo Tafuri, *Architecture and Utopia: Design and Capitalist Development* (Bari, 1973, English trs Cambridge, MA: MIT Press, 1976).

Ornament and Subjectivity

2

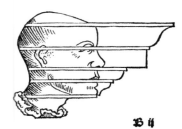

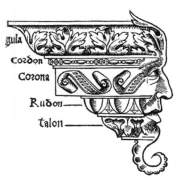

Architecture does not necessarily 'speak' as Etienne-Louis Boullée, Claude-Nicolas Ledoux and other late 18th-century architects had tried to suggest. Rather, it possesses an expressive character; it conveys affects, emotions and thoughts. In contrast to nature, architectural form is entirely intentional and its effects purposefully created. It implies authorship as well as the existence of a public. By whom is architecture designed and produced? For whom is it meant? To put it differently, who are the subjects involved in the production and reception of architectural works?

From the Renaissance to the dawn of Modernism, ornament played a key role in the answers provided to this set of questions. It raised the issue of the identity and role of the designer, whether this be the high-profile architect described by theorists in their treatises or a mere entrepreneur, master mason or even carpenter. It reflected the place allotted to artists and artisans, sculptors, painters, joiners or plasterers, in the production of architectural works. It said something crucial about the nature of the relation between buildings, clients and passers-by. This chapter is devoted to the discussion of the ways traditional décor revealed itself inseparable from the various subjects of architecture.

The Visage of Architecture

Before entering into the details of this discussion, it is worth noting how architectural ornament also engaged the issue of subjectivity at a broader and more generic level. Through ornamentation, buildings themselves seemed to acquire something like a facial appearance, a personality, which enabled them to enter into dialogue with human beings.[1] In her classic study of the theoretical foundations of Western architecture, *The Rule and the Model*, French philosopher Françoise Choay insists on the conversational character of the discipline, as envisaged by its Renaissance founding fathers beginning with Leon Battista Alberti.[2] This dialogic character was actually inseparable from ornamentation, which was supposed to give distinctive features to architectural works so that they could enter into a conversation with man.

In one of the drawings of his treatise of architecture, the Renaissance Italian architect and engineer Francesco di Giorgio Martini superimposes the head of a young man on the details of a cornice, as if the various mouldings that constitute it were literally comparable to the features of a face. 'Having measured very many other cornices I have found plenty which do have the proportion of a head,' he writes. On his drawing, the face of the man is shown in profile just like the mouldings of the cornice. This anthropocentric analogy would remain an enduring feature of the Vitruvian tradition. Similar representations are used by Spanish theorist Diego de Sagredo in his 1526 *Medidas del Romano* (Measures of the Roman), one of the first architectural treatises published in vernacular language outside Italy. 'The Ancients arranged the moldings of the cornice to fit over a man's face,' explains Sagredo. Later, Gian Lorenzo Bernini follows the same principle in one of his drawings.[3] A striking 18th-century instance of the parallel between mouldings and facial features can be found in Jacques-François Blondel's 1771–7 *Cours d'Architecture* (Course of Architecture). Blondel's purpose is to make his reader aware of the profound differences of inspiration between the entablatures of Palladio, Scamozzi and Vignola. According to him, these differences are very well conveyed by comparing the human profiles that they evoke. Whereas Palladio's entablature reminds him of a mature bearded head, Scamozzi's and above all Vignola's profiles suggest more juvenile figures.[4]

To enrich the meaning of this recurring analogy, it is useful to return to the Greek etymological kinship between cosmos and cosmetics, between the general order of things and techniques of body ornament, which range from dress to make-up. The cosmos represents the universe revealing itself as an

Previous page: Diego de Sagredo, profiles of mouldings with human heads, from *Medidas del Romano*, 1526.
The association between human heads and mouldings suggests that architectural décor is actually looking at the observer. The suggestion is even stronger with the second image in which the visage protrudes on the right, as an exact equivalent of the architectural profiles on the left.

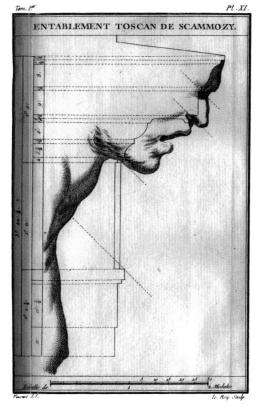

Tam. Iᵉʳ   Pl. XI.

ENTABLEMENT TOSCAN DE SCAMMOZY.

Jacques-François Blondel, Tuscan entablature of Scamozzi, from *Cours d'architecture*, 1771–7. Blondel uses the analogy with the human face to convey the specificity of Scamozzi's interpretation of the orders. The 18th-century architectural concept of character finds here a literal illustration.

ordered whole imparted with beauty. Cosmetics refer to the various adornments that enhance the look of an individual. Both incorporate the notion of harmonious features becoming perceivable through a process of emergence.

In modern English, the term cosmetics has become closely associated with make-up. From creams to powders, from lotions to lipsticks, cosmetics are meant to enhance the physical appearance beginning with the face. Good make-up constitutes both a disguise and a revelation. It may be interpreted as a kind of mask as well as a means to disclose the true personality of an individual. As anthropologists are well aware, this is actually a general property of masks: they conceal and reveal at the same time. 'In addition to disguise and transformation, revealing identity is another reason for masking,' so the curators of an exhibition on masks as faces of culture remind us.[5] Masks and make-up can be seen as human extensions of the biological process that led selected living beings to acquire a face.

Where ornament is concerned, it becomes tempting to relate it to a cosmetic dimension characteristic of certain buildings and spaces. Transfigured by architecture in an almost literal sense, these buildings and spaces acquire something like a visage, hence the impression, which one experiences at times, that they are about to 'speak'. More common is the feeling that they are looking at us while we examine them. Architecture is what happens when buildings begin to acquire a visage; ornament is like the mask or make-up that participates in the emergence of this visage.

In the first volume of *Spheres*, his monumental and baroque trilogy on modernity, German philosopher Peter Sloterdijk insists on the fact that human faces exist only in relation to other faces.[6] According to him, this relation generates an interfacial space or rather sphere, to use Sloterdijk's vocabulary, which is constitutive of intersubjectivity. Part of the ambition of ornamented architecture is to engage with humans in a somewhat similar way, that is, to create connection between visages that gives birth to an intersubjective sphere. This engagement is made possible by the fact that the visage of an adorned building is actually obtained as a composition or superimposition of the faces of all the actors that have contributed to its design, construction and use. Each one has left a feature or trace, some highly visible, others almost imperceptible. They are present at the surface of the building, through its ornaments, like the profiles of the heads that gave their character to the mouldings of Francesco di Giorgio Martini, Diego de Sagredo, Gian Lorenzo Bernini or Jacques-François Blondel.

The Architect, between Rules and Invention

The architect is among the first concerned by ornament. Vitruvius and his followers entrust him with the conception of décor as well as with the task of supervising its realisation. But a number of problems arise almost immediately. The first has to do with the level of detail into which the architect is supposed to venture. Can he limit himself to general indications regarding ornamentation or must he provide precise drawings of everything, including mouldings? The question had to be answered by each designer individually. In early modern Europe, the issue proved all the more crucial given that architecture could be practised by amateurs like Christopher Wren, an English physicist, or Claude Perrault, a French doctor. Could amateurs devote the same degree of attention to ornamental details as professional designers and builders? The desire to counterbalance the power of entrepreneurs, artisans and artists in charge of the concrete realisation of buildings could have been one of the motives behind Perrault's proposal for a radical standardisation of the architectural orders exposed in his 1683 *Ordonnance des Cinq Espèces de Colonnes selon la Méthode des Anciens* (Ordonnance for the Five Kinds of Columns after the Method of the Ancients).[7] Before him, this preoccupation had already accounted for the success of Giacomo Barozzi da Vignola's system of proportions and moulding profiles – much simpler than those of its rivals – among French architects.

A second problem reveals itself as even more fundamental. It concerns the level of personal expression deemed acceptable when designing ornaments, a source of possible tension between individual inspiration and rules, between the pleasure of creation and the knowledge of the principles. Among the arts, architecture has always been somewhat peculiar in its insistence upon rules. Until the end of the 18th century, these rules were easy to identify: the discipline was supposed to follow the Greco-Roman paradigm exposed by Vitruvius and formally re-established during the Renaissance. Rules became less clear during the 19th century. Actually, architecture has not followed any unified set of principles since the demise of the Vitruvian tradition, but the desire for rules has remained intact.

Although Vitruvian rules did not strictly prescribe the precise nature, position and appearance of ornaments, they nevertheless gave a number of decisive indications about their design and use. Overall restraint appeared as a key principle. A harmonious coordination between whole and parts through the use of ratios and proportions represented another fundamental aspect of the Vitruvian legacy. These indications were further elaborated by authors of treatises, beginning with Andrea Palladio, Vincenzo Scamozzi and Giacomo Barozzi da Vignola in Italy. A potentially troubling issue lay in the fact that these authors gave slightly different versions of key elements such as the proportions of the orders and the profiles of the various mouldings that accompanied the use of columns and pilasters. Jacques-François Blondel's evocation of heads to convey these differences indicated their ties to an individual dimension, which rules were theoretically not supposed to allow. The diversity of Greco-Roman ornaments, beginning with the proportions of the orders, constituted another puzzling fact noted by those who attempted precisely to draw ancient monuments. At the end of the 17th century, French architect Antoine Desgodets gave the definitive demonstration of this diversity in his 1682 *Les Edifices Antiques de Rome* (The Ancient

Sebastiano Serlio, rustic gate, from *Extraordinario Libro*, 1551.
Part of the invention lies in the heterodox combination of Doric and Corinthian elements. The invasive presence of the rustication challenges also the received principles of architecture.

Buildings of Rome), which provided Perrault with a decisive argument for making alterations of his own to the Vitruvian canon, since this canon had not been used that rigorously by the Romans themselves.

Such variations from one author or building to another meant that the power of rules was necessarily counterbalanced by some latitude left to the designer in their interpretation. Where would be the art otherwise? This latitude or licence rapidly became a major theme of architectural investigation, since it afforded the possibility of individual expression. Furthermore, licence was especially noticeable when applied to architectural décor. More than the overall proportions that followed relatively restrictive guidelines, the use of ornament seemed to obey a looser set of recommendations.

Sebastiano Serlio was among the principal Renaissance theorists of the tricky notion of licence and its application to ornament. Two dimensions were especially at stake for him: one was variation; the other, the integration of parts borrowed from different decorative contexts. In a notable passage of his fourth book on architecture devoted to the rustic order, he elaborates on this integration in the following terms:

> In addition, without distancing oneself from what was done by the Ancients, one could also mix and connect this Rustic *opera* with the Doric, and also with the Ionic, and sometimes with the Corinthian, according to the wishes of who wanted to satisfy a personal fancy. This however, would be, one must own, more *di licentia* than according to reason: because the architect must proceed with great modesty and reserve, especially in public buildings and those of *gravità*, where it is always praiseworthy to respect *decoro*.[8]

Everything, or almost, is said in this passage: the possibility of departing occasionally from the rules; the deeply personal motive that accounts for this departure; and the tension between reason, social decorum and fancy that it generates. Mannerism, this transitional phase between Renaissance and Baroque, was based on multiple licences like those taken by Giulio Romano at Palazzo del Te in Mantua (1526–34).

However, licence was only the beginning of the problem. For a larger question loomed behind the play upon variation and mixing of parts: that of invention. As Alina Payne notes, Serlio's licences are often fully-fledged inventions, especially in the fourth of his 'extraordinary' books on architecture, even if his use of the latter term remains limited.[9] In France,

Giulio Romano, Palazzo del Te, Mantua, 1526–34. The Palazzo del Te is one of the finest examples of Mannerist architecture. The play on the limits of the Vitruvian order pervades the entire building. At the main entrance, the rhythm of pilasters is disrupted by unconventional rustication. Licences are even more conspicuous inside the courtyard where some of the triglyphs of the frieze seem to have dropped from their initial position.

Philibert Delorme appears as the great Renaissance theorist of invention.[10] The word is present in the title of one of his two treatises: his 1561 *Nouvelles Inventions pour Bien Bastir et à Petits Frais* (New Inventions to Build Well and at Small Expense), devoted to an innovative carpentry assemblage that would be rediscovered in the late 18th century. It likewise appears repeatedly in his main theoretical work, his 1567 first volume on architecture. In this treatise, invention is invoked to characterise various proposals, which he presents as path-breaking ideas and realisations. Although Delorme's favourite invention is an original design method applied to determine the complex geometry of the conic vault supporting a suspended cabinet at the castle of Anet (1552), many others are ornamental, like his proposal for the Ionic capital or his series of designs for new types of columns without equivalent in Ancient architecture. The architect had used such columns at the Tuileries Palace built for Queen Catherine de Medici (started in 1564).

With Delorme, the individual and subjective dimension of ornamental invention is especially conspicuous. His contemporary Bernard Palissy criticised the exaggerated sense of self-importance that led him to claim the title of 'god of the masons or architects'.[11] Delorme was, incidentally, the first French architect to have commissioned a portrait of himself. At the very end of his first volume on architecture, the alliance between the subjective and the ornamental is admirably conveyed by two famous engravings representing respectively the bad and the good architect. Whereas the bad architect wanders in a barren landscape dominated by a gloomy medieval castle, the good architect enjoys the pleasures of a garden. Beautiful buildings rise on each side, their ornaments echoing the productions of nature. The parallel is epitomised by the presence of cornucopias both on the ground and on top of one of the buildings, as if fruits and flowers were at the origin of decoration. Revealingly, in addition to lacking hands because he does not know how to make something useful, the bad architect has no recognisable features; he is deprived of eyes, nose, mouth and ears, whereas the good architect has a visage. The latter is, moreover, engaged in a dialogue with a young disciple who turns his own face towards him. With their windows wide open like eyes surveying the scene, the nearby buildings seem to look on this conversation with benevolence. They are actually part of it. Good, adorned architecture contributes to Sloterdijk's notion of an interfacial sphere.

With his apologue of the bad and good architect, Delorme raises a question that will preoccupy theorists for a long time: that of the personal qualities associated with invention, and in particular with ornamental invention. For many Vitruvian authors, imagination and genius play a crucial role in the capacity to invent new formal combinations. But these qualities can lead to exaggerations and even aberrations. From the Renaissance to the 18th century, warning against this potential danger was common in architectural theory. Etienne-Louis

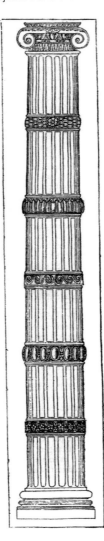

Philibert Delorme, Ionic column, from *Le Premier Tome de l'Architecture*, 1567.
The banded column that the Ancients did not use is presented as an important invention by Delorme. As often with the architect, the invention mixes technological and aesthetic concerns. The bands make the masonry joints between the various parts of the shaft less visible. Delorme employed this sort of column at the Tuileries Palace, started in 1564.

Boullée still cautions against misuse of imagination and genius in his essay on architecture begun during the last decade of the Ancien Régime, despite his definition of architecture as a production of images and his insistence on the necessity for the architect to show genius in almost every circumstance. One of his targets is Giovanni Battista Piranesi, whose creations he sees as typical products of a disorganised mind. He characterises them further as extravagances made of the same substance as dreams.[12] However, what renders delicate this kind of attack against misguided imagination and genius is the assumption that both are ultimately rooted in nature: imagination, because of the predominant theory of imitation that postulates that the copy of nature is the source of art and architecture; genius, because it appears as a natural disposition of the mind. How could the lessons of nature go wrong? Ornamental invention reveals one of the most fundamental ambiguities of the theoretical foundations of the architectural discipline, an ambiguity rooted in the characterisation of the ideal designer as an inventive genius following the dictates of nature.

During the second half of the 18th century, Piranesi gave a new urgency to the debate on this issue with his engravings as well as his polemics with French collector and connoisseur, Pierre-Jean Mariette. In the so-called Greco-Roman quarrel, deciding on whether the Greeks had the advantage over the Romans in terms of artistic excellence, Mariette had taken the side of the former, accusing the latter of having produced 'nothing that is not laden with superfluous and gratuitous ornament'.[13] As Tafuri noted, Piranesi's answer goes beyond the archaeological dimension of the quarrel by challenging the very foundation of the Vitruvian tradition in the name of unfettered imagination.[14] Nowhere is the challenge made more evident than in the compositions that illustrate his answer to Mariette. In these compositions, ornament proliferates in a way that announces the possibility of relating it to a decorative impulse.[15] Its accumulation threatens the notions of order and proportion that lie at the core of Vitruvianism. Also challenged is the ideal of a coherent language of architecture based on a limited set of formal elements. The trajectory leading from Piranesi's 1743 *Prima Parte di Architetture, e Prospettive* (Part One of Architecture and Perspectives), to his 1769 *Diverse Maniere d'Adornare I Cammini ed Ogni Altra Parte degli Edifizi* (Diverse Manners of Ornamenting Chimneys and All Other Parts of Houses), is marked by a spectacular rise in the range and variety of ornaments as well as in their modes of assemblage, which hinders any attempt to circumscribe

Giovanni Battista Piranesi, imaginary architectural composition from the *Parere su l'Architettura*, after 1767.

This composition and the next are part of a series of six plates added to the dialogue *Parere su l'Architettura*. In this series, Piranesi reaches a level of personal expression hardly compatible with the Vitruvian tradition. In the centre, a quotation from French theorist Julien-David Le Roy, a major advocate of Greek artistic supremacy, is used against his author. It says 'So as not to make this sublime art where one would only copy without choice.' Piranesi's unorthodox composition is definitely not a copy.

architecture within the confines of predetermined vocabulary and syntax. Imagination and genius, two qualities evidently possessed at the highest level by the 'wicked architect' evoked by Tafuri, are almost about to overthrow the rules of the discipline.[16]

As discussed later in this chapter, the existence of an ornamental impulse irreducible to the play of predetermined rules was largely acknowledged in the 19th century. By the same token, the crisis epitomised by Piranesi was

Giovanni Battista Piranesi,
imaginary architectural
composition from the
Parere su l'Architettura,
after 1767.
The last plate of the series
displays the facade of a
temple. Taken from Sallust,
a Latin inscription at the
top reads 'They despise my
novelty, I their timidity.'
In this composition, the
ornamental frieze subverts
almost completely the
tectonic order of the
colonnade and its pediment.
Borrowed from Egypt,
Greece and Rome, the
ornaments also present
masonic connotations.

not to find a definitive solution before Loos's drastic dismissal of ornament.
Until the dawn of Modernism, ornamentation remained nonetheless a key
index of the genius, which great architects are supposed to display. There is
perhaps no better illustration of this connection than Frank Lloyd Wright's
development on the 'adventure of the mind' that represented ornament for
his former employer and mentor, Louis Sullivan:

> Ah, that supreme, erotic, high adventure of the mind that was his ornament!
> Often I would see him, his back bent over his drawing board, intent upon
> what? I knew his symbolism – I caught his feelings as he worked. A Casanova
> on his rounds? Beside this sensuous master of adventure with tenuous, vibrant,
> plastic form, Casanova was a duffer; Gil Blas a torn chapeau; Boccaccio's
> imagination no higher than a stable-boy's. Compared to this high quest
> the Don's was as Sancho Panza's ass. The soul of Rabelais alone could have
> understood and would have called him a brother. How often I have held his
> cloak and sword while he adventured in the realm within, to win his mistress;
> and while he wooed the mistress, I would woo the maid![17]

This adventure of the mind leads ultimately to the partial embodiment of the architect in the ornament. The evocative power of adorned architecture comes from the feeling of a personal presence that expresses itself through the relation between décor and overall ambience. Modernism breaks with this type of presence both crystallised and diffuse, concentrated in specific parts of the buildings and spread throughout space. With the disappearance of traditional ornament, the signature of the designer becomes more global, similar to a vital inspiration, which permeates everything but runs the risk of becoming more anonymous. To be sure, dramatic spatial sequences, light effects, tectonic articulations, material textures and even furniture can play the role formerly devoted to ornamentation. But they do not look at the spectator in the way ornament does. To put it differently, the architect is still embodied in the building, but his body has lost the familiar face of the humanist subject.[18]

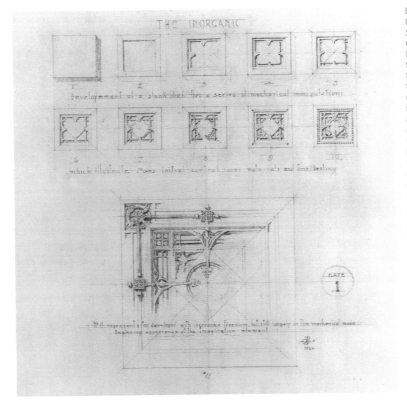

Louis Sullivan, 'The Inorganic', drawing for *A System of Architectural Ornament*, 1922. Louis Sullivan's ambition to theorise graphically the principles at work in the composition of his ornaments begins by the inorganic, or how to develop a blank block through controlled manipulations. Control, energy, power, but also impulse, will and freedom, appear as key words throughout the commentary of the 20 plates of *A System of Architectural Ornament*. As Frank Llyod Wright aptly observed, what is at stake is an adventure of the creative mind.

Artists, Craftsmen and the Fabrication of Ornament

Until the 19th century and the industrialisation of decorative elements, ornament was usually produced by hand. This involved a whole range of subjects other than the architect: artists, craftsmen, entrepreneurs, with the additional complexity that we have already mentioned, namely that these figures often took part in the design. In many cases, the architect, when there was an architect, limited himself to the overall organisation of exterior and interior décor. The collaborative dimension of ornamentation was seldom acknowledged by theorists. As historian of art and architecture Katie Scott notes in her book on Rococo Parisian interiors: 'in order for decoration to work – to command the patronage of the great – post-Renaissance theory demanded that it should deflect attention from the technologies of its manufacture and obscure the antagonism around which its production was organized'.[19]

There are, however, exceptions to this attitude of denial. In his writings, Philibert Delorme indirectly acknowledges the importance of craftsmen and workers through his repeated complaints against their malpractices.[20] Delorme's ultimate ambition was to control completely the production of buildings, including the details of ornamentation. Yet in most cases, a negotiation took place between the various partners involved in the process leading from design to construction. A plate illustrating the lectures on architecture of Augustin-Charles d'Aviler, one of the most influential French treatises of the late 17th century, reveals the strategic importance of ornament in this negotiation.[21] It presents the various types of mouldings along two columns: one indicates the names given by craftsmen and workers; the other, the terms used by architectural theorists. The sharp contrast between the former and latter could hardly be greater. When craftsmen speak of *baguette* and *boudin*, fillet and roll moulding, theorists mention astragal and torus. But they need to understand each other so that construction can take place, hence d'Aviler's plate. More generally, ornament often coincides with professional boundaries. At this level also, it marks a threshold leading from one culture to another. This explains its importance in the development of professional education for workers in the late 18th and early 19th centuries.[22]

Despite the recurring tensions between architects, artists and craftsmen, and although negotiation was unavoidable on issues like ornament, concrete problems of fabrication remained for a long time external to the core of the architectural discipline, like a potentially threatening issue perceived only through peripheral vision. During the first half of the 19th century, industrialisation changed everything. It placed fabrication right in the centre of the cone of vision of architectural theorists and practitioners, and this for

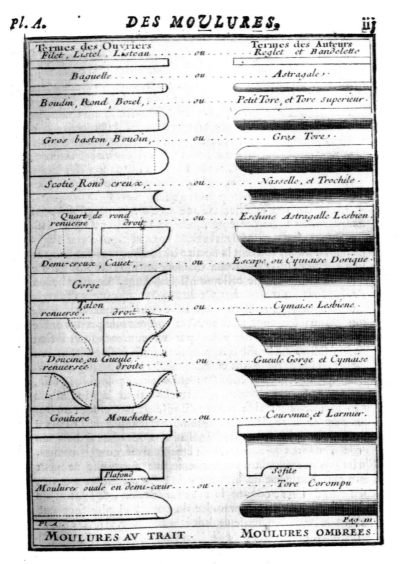

Augustin-Charles d'Aviler, mouldings, from *Cours d'Architecture*, 1691.
On the left the profiles of the mouldings with the terms used by the workers, on the right the same profiles with the terms used by the authors of architectural treatises. Revealingly, on the side of the authors, the profiles are shadowed, thus suggesting that proper appreciation of their effects requires theoretical grounding.

a variety of reasons. The possibility of prefabricating ornamental elements played a decisive role. From modest terracotta medallions to large statues, like the caryatids produced by the Virebent workshop in the city of Toulouse in south-west France, these prefabricated elements raised the question of the direction that architecture was actually taking.[23] Could one envisage that design and construction would eventually revolve around the assemblage of ready-made elements produced in workshops or large factories? Even more than the standardisation of iron and steel structural parts, which were often concealed in the thickness of walls and floors, in the case of ordinary buildings at least, the highly visible prefabrication of ornament seemed to pave the way for a drastic evolution of design and building processes. Ironically, many questions addressed by 19th-century architects through ornament were further investigated by Modernism via the abandonment of traditional architectural décor. For the 19th-century designer, industrialisation was very present at the level of ornamentation. It is only during the first decades of the 20th century that it became limited only to structure and building technologies.

Despite the promises of industrialisation, hand-produced ornament remained predominant in countries like France that built in stone. From the New Louvre of Napoleon III to ordinary apartment buildings, the realisation of Haussmannian Paris mobilised an army of stone-cutters and sculptors, not to mention the numerous painters entrusted with the decoration of all sorts of interior venues, from railway-station waiting rooms to bourgeois salons. The pervasive presence of skilled labour brought up another disturbing question, that of its rising cost. From Eugène-Emmanuel Viollet-le-Duc to Auguste Choisy, French Rationalist theorists were obsessed by what they perceived as an inexorable trend that could threaten the very foundations of architecture. This led them to pay keen attention to questions of standardisation, especially in the tectonic realm, standardisation distinct from mere industrial production since it characterised already pre-industrial styles like Greek or Gothic. For Viollet-le-Duc, one of the major interests of the lancet arch used in Gothic architecture lay in the fact that it allowed for the standardised manufacture of voussoirs. With the Rationalists starts the evolution that will eventually lead to the privilege given to structural considerations by Modernism: hence their presentation as forerunners of the Modern Movement by historians such as Reyner Banham or Kenneth Frampton.[24]

However, the Rationalist attitude towards ornament should have led to more circumspection in asserting such filiation. Although Viollet-le-Duc

A 19th-century house in the city of Montauban, south-west of France. The facade of this house, probably built during the first half of the 19th century, is adorned with prefabricated elements. The most remarkable are the three white terracotta caryatid figures produced by the Virebent workshop in Toulouse. Later in the century, terracotta prefabricated ornaments would be extensively used in all sorts of urban constructions, including the first skyscrapers in the United States.

repeatedly suggests that ornament should appear, at least ideally, as a logical consequence of a fundamental tectonic inspiration (this is among the reasons that Greek architecture and, above all, the Gothic are so remarkable in his eyes), his own practice of ornamentation differs profoundly from this reductive stance. To the contrary, Viollet-le-Duc's ornaments seem on many occasions to obey a vital and wild impulse, like the foliage that adorns his lectern for the cathedral Notre-Dame de Paris (1868).[25] Because of the vital

Louis-Emile Durandelle, 'Frise et Corniche de la Scène', frieze and cornice of the stage, from Charles Garnier, *Le Nouvel Opéra de Paris: Sculpture Ornementale*, 1876.
A sculptor at work on Garnier's new Opera. From ordinary buildings to exceptional monuments, Haussmannian Paris appears as a giant architectural and urban décor based on the extensive use of stone sculpture.

character of many of his ornamental designs, he appears more in tune with Art Nouveau than with Modernism proper. In addition, contrary there again to a commonly held assumption, Viollet-le-Duc is not at all insensitive to the creative input of artists and artisans in architectural décor. Choisy is even more explicit on this question. According to a passage of his 1883 *Art de Bâtir chez les Byzantins* (The Art of Building of the Byzantines), part of what makes Greek and Byzantine art attractive lies in the latitude left to the craftsmen to express themselves. 'Each sculptor has his stone and is free to manage its ornaments; one feels that the architect wanted to tie him to the common work by leaving him the possibility of leaving a trace of his participation,' states Choisy.[26] Beside the cost of labour involved in its production, the creative dimension of hand-made ornament represents another motive of interest for 19th-century architectural theorists and practitioners.

No other theorist goes further down this path than John Ruskin. His radical take on the importance of the craftsman's hand in the quality and expressivity of ornament profoundly marked subsequent architectural attitudes towards décor, beginning with the Arts and Crafts Movement. For Ruskin, ornament is primarily meant to give pleasure, and through this pleasure it conveys a higher realm of spiritual values. But this double function requires the craftsman to be animated by a mix of enjoyment and inspiration similar to that subsequently experienced by the admirer of his work.

Eugène-Emmanuel Viollet-le-Duc, preparatory drawing for the lectern of Notre-Dame de Paris, March 1868.
In many of Viollet-le-Duc's drawings, ornament seems animated with an existence of its own. Here it evokes some fantastic form of organic life, a crossbreed of foliage and starfish or even octopus. The austere lessons of Rationalism remain very far from this ornamental surge that announces Art Nouveau.

Ruskin proves equally influential in his advocacy of irregularity and, even, imperfection as the true markers of living authenticity as opposed to the inanimate precision of the machine. Following the political historian and essayist Thomas Carlyle, he is appalled by mechanisation that he interprets as a profound dehumanisation of society. In his eyes, such dehumanisation is epitomised by industrial ornament. Its repetitive character, so different from the uniqueness of every living form from plants to animals, becomes synonymous with the enslavement of men. True ornament possesses a singularity linked to the deliberations and hesitations of the mind and hand working together. It is not servile imitation but re-creation of life.

John Ruskin, 'Part of the Cathedral of St Lo, Normandy', from *The Seven Lamps of Architecture*, 1849. The autonomous life of ornament reaches its climax with John Ruskin. Away from the 'fallacy' of the substitution of cast or machine work for that of the hand, traditional ornament bears the mark of 'human labour and care spent upon it'.

Like Viollet-le-Duc, Ruskin appears as an admirer of Gothic, but whereas the French theorist is primarily interested in the overall design in which he detects the premises of modern rationalisation, his English counterpart sees something profoundly different: the possibility of a collective work of art preserving the freedom of all the individuals that partake in it. From such a perspective, ornament no longer represents a mere threshold leading from one professional culture to another. It marks the entrance of a realm of inspiration, both highly individual and in tune with the general spirit that permeates the architectural work. As for Viollet-le-Duc, he is far less interested in the craftsman even if he recognises his contribution. He believes in the supremacy of a master-builder figure who is both in charge of the overall design and the promoter of the best methods to realise it, methods including standardisation of components like the voussoirs of the lancet arch.

With Ruskin, the full extent of the contribution of the craftsman was finally recognised in architecture. Prior to him, such evolution had already taken place in domains ranging from joinery to textile design, as the development of specialised drawing classes for craftsmen and workers in countries such as France or England demonstrates.[27] This recognition led to major architectural realisations like Thomas Newenham Deane and Benjamin Woodward's Oxford University Museum of Natural History (1860), which benefited from direct suggestions by John Ruskin.[28] The building attempts to reconcile the use of iron, the emblematic material of industrialisation, with an elaborate décor entrusted to the Irish sculptors James and John O'Shea and their nephew Edward Whelan. In addition to the official decorative programme, which comprises statues of eminent men of science as well as columns, each made of different British stones, lively sculptures of plants and animals also adorn the construction. Despite the sculptors' initial ambitions, the University would not allow them to repeat the kind of pranks they had played at the Dublin Kildare Street Club (1860) where the club members are depicted as monkeys playing billiards. Even at its climax, Ruskinian ornamental freedom has its limits.

The episode would be relatively short-lived anyhow, despite the attempts of the Arts and Crafts Movement led by William Morris to emulate the mode of production of medieval guilds. Like Pugin before him, Morris was confronted

The sculptor James O'Shea at work on carvings for the Oxford University Museum of Natural History, 1860.
Inspired by John Ruskin's theories, Thomas Newenham Deane and Benjamin Woodward – the architects of the Oxford University Museum – tried to recapture part of the creative freedom that made traditional ornament so appealing, according to the author of *The Seven Lamps of Architecture*. This led them to commission James and John O'Shea and their nephew Edward Whelan to carve the elaborate décor of the museum.

with the fundamental ambiguity of such an attempt. Instead of bearing the mark of the inspired freedom of the craftsman, the designs of his firm appear as the products of a more traditional organisation. Often entrusted to artists like Edward Burne-Jones or William Morris himself, they do not leave much freedom to those in charge of their realisation.

The legacy of the Arts and Crafts Movement to Modernism is manifold. It includes the ideal of a wholly designed environment as well as the project to reform industry to enhance the quality of everyday objects. But although the influence of Ruskin's and Morris's ambition to restore the prerogatives of the craftsman can still be detected in the fondness with which some architects such as Le Corbusier chose to display the trace of the hand of the worker in some of their buildings, Modernism as a whole tried to reduce as much as possible the latitude left to him. With this reduction, presented by its proponents as a major step towards the transformation of construction into a precision industry, part of the pleasurable dimension associated with the production of architecture dissipated.

From Clients to Passers-by

For whom is architectural ornament meant? This question introduces a whole range of new subjects, from the client to the simple passer-by as well as from the living to the dead, for traditional ornament does not only frame and reflect what is happening around and inside buildings. One of its roles also consists in reminding the living of the passage of time and of the existence of those who preceded them. Just like writing, ornament is inseparable from both present experience and memory.

According to the Vitruvian tradition, ornament was supposed to convey information about the nature of the building and the rank of its owner. From the Renaissance to the late 18th century, this function was rooted in the notion of an almost one-to-one system of correspondence between the gradation of architectural décors and the pyramid of conditions that characterised pre-industrial societies. The use of the same word 'order' to characterise the fundamental types of architectural ornamentation and the main social divisions inherited from the Middle Ages – the clergy, the nobility and the third estate – proves especially revealing in this respect. Architectural ornament was not only a marker of social status. Its levels of richness and sophistication were supposed to come from the same source, which had given birth to the various social distinctions. Ultimately, they all derived from a natural course of the universe instituted by God who, according to French 17th-century theologian and philosopher Jacques-Bénigne Bossuet, had created the world by establishing the principles of order and proportion.[29]

However, just as the quest for self-expression of the designer was not always compatible with the general principles of the

William Morris, design for 'Vine' wallpaper, 1873–4. Morris's design is emblematic of the fundamental ambiguity of the Arts and Crafts Movement towards workers. On the one hand, the ambition is to re-create a collective spirit of creation uniting designers and makers. On the other hand, the designer does not leave much leeway to those in charge of the implementation of his ideas.

architectural discipline, the aspirations of the client could reveal themselves contradictory to the plans of the architect and the rules he tried to follow. The higher the rank of the patron, the greater the probability that such tension could arise. Indeed, the temptation was great to consider the architect as the provider of a service rather than the keeper of rules that transcended the will of his employer. The Marquis de Lassay, a French nobleman, declared for instance in 1756: 'I find all constraint, all subservience insupportable; the very slightest is painful; I use a doctor, a lawyer, an architect as a tool; and for nothing would I suffer that they exert the least authority over me; I always reserve the right to judge whether that they tell me is good or bad.'[30]

At the time of this statement, which equated the architect to a mere tool to be disregarded at will, the tension between the aspirations of the client and the rules that the architect was tempted to impose on him had reached a new stage. This was linked to the development of an interior decoration that was supposed to correspond not only to the public social status of its owner but also to some key features of his private character. On the eve of the 18th century, Charles Perrault, the brother of Claude, had foreseen such evolution in a passage of a manuscript entitled *Pensées Chrétiennes* (Christian Thoughts), in which he opposed exterior and interior decoration:

> Architectural ornaments must all be serious outside buildings, because they
> are seen by all kinds of people all the time, and one owes as a mark of respect
> to the public to appear always proper in front of it. Architectural ornaments
> can be bizarre and even grotesque inside, where the only ones to enter are
> those whom we authorize to do so and at chosen times.[31]

In addition to the client and the contrast between exterior demeanour and intimate behaviour, which architectural décors could convey by means of the opposition between the serious and the bizarre, Perrault also had in mind the simple passer-by. Constitutive of the public, the passer-by ranks among the addressees of architectural ornament. On the eve of the Enlightenment, the importance of the public was on the rise in direct relation to a new concern for civic values that would eventually lead to debates in the second half of the 18th century on the moral utility of architecture. But this rise was once again counterbalanced by new perspectives offered by the relation between spatial and psychological interiority. Rococo experiments explored this path before the mid-century reaction against what would often be presented as 'excess': a formal overflow as much as a door opened on the possibility of subjective outpouring.

Joseph Michael Gandy, *View of the Dome area of John Soane's House looking East*, 1811. In this dramatic view, the Piranesian accumulation of architectural fragments appears all the more spectacular as it rises from a lower level that evokes a catacomb. The exaggerated perspective is also reminiscent of Piranesi's play on unusual points of view.

Germain Boffrand, Salon de la Princesse of the Hôtel de Soubise, Paris, 1737–40.
Designed by architect Germain Boffrand, the oval Salon de la Princesse of the Hôtel de Soubise is one of the finest Rococo interiors in Paris. The décor carries clear female connotations with sculpted cupids by Jean-Baptiste Lemoyne and paintings by Charles-Joseph Natoire illustrating the adventures of Psyche.

Beyond the Greek reaction of the 1750s and its return to codes of interior decoration in tune with the respect owed to the public, to use Perrault's formula, the desire to convey essential features of one's character through inside ornaments would continue to haunt late 18th- and 19th-century architecture. In the case of upper-class women's apartments, this desire was especially present in the famous boudoirs, which were meant to host the most private part of their lives.[32] More generally, the increasing specialisation of rooms that characterised the evolution of dwelling during this period reinforced the possibility of an interior decoration suited to the aspirations of its occupants.[33]

Such an adequacy reached one of its most spectacular climaxes with the creation of John Soane's house (1792–1837), which relied on Piranesian techniques of archaeological accumulation and collage to transform a relatively modest London residence into a fantastic museum. Soane's house appears as much as a journey inside the mind of its owner as a travel in space and time from Ancient Egypt to 19th-century England.

If Soane's museum remains exceptional as the work of one of the most talented architects of his generation, the age of industry was marked by a multiplication of fantastic interiors, the rich ornamentation of which was supposed to mirror the psyche of their owners, to evoke their life-defining experiences, their travels and encounters, as well as to convey their aspirations towards an even richer and more varied form of existence. Located in Rochefort, a French port city on the Atlantic coast, the house of novelist Pierre Loti (1895–1923) hides behind a banal facade a series of extravagantly decorated rooms. One of them evokes a mosque, another a Turkish salon. The visitor also passes through Gothic and Renaissance rooms. Like Soane's museum, Loti's house aesthetically combines spatial and temporal contrasts.

Throughout the 19th century, the conception of the house or apartment as a reflection of the inner self and its aspirations achieved primarily through ornamentation appears as a paroxysmal form of the bourgeois taste for heavily furnished and decorated interiors. In his writings on 19th-century modernity, Walter Benjamin defines this type of space as 'the étui of the private individual', one of the places where the phantasmagoria of capitalist society develops as an antidote to the perceived banality of a world based on commodity fetishism.[34] In such a perspective, interior ornament appears both as a commodity that can be accumulated like any other one, and as the expression of the desire to transcend the commodification of the world, this very desire that Benjamin denounces as an illusion. For Modernist architects, the break with ornamentation represents not only an aesthetic decision. It is also rooted in the project to dispel the phantasmagoria to reveal the harsh but also stimulating truth of the industrial age. This project figures among the key aspects of the German quest for a *Neue Sachlichkeit*, a New Objectivity.

Turkish Salon of Pierre Loti's House in Rochefort, after 1895.
French novelist Julien Viaud (1850–1923), better known by his pen name, Pierre Loti, spent a large part of his life transforming the house he was born in into an elaborate suite of décors, most of them referring to the Orient, one of his major sources of inspiration.

With the ban on richly ornamented interiors came the implicit condemnation of a certain type of identification between the inhabitant and the space he occupies that was now deemed excessive, if not pathological. Yet the tradition exemplified by John Soane or Pierre Loti has nevertheless survived the Modernist ban, especially in countries like the United States where the single-family house has remained the dominant form of dwelling. Buffalo-based artist Dennis Maher fits neatly within this tradition with his extraordinary Fargo House filled with collections, constructions, assemblages and collages that possess an ornamental turn.

From Soane and Loti to Maher, what seems additionally at stake is not only the question of ornamented interior space as a reflection of the personality of the owner of the house. With their fragments borrowed from ancient or recent history, from Greco-Roman temples or medieval mosques to suburban yard sales (a major source of supply for Maher's creations), these interiors also raise issues related to memory: a dimension all the more evident in the case of Soane's house in that it was conceived almost from the start as the combination of a residence and a museum.[35] More generally, ornament not only says something about the present, it also plays a commemorative role.

Harold Sutton Palmer, the Drawing Room, Wickham Hall, Kent, 1897.
This overcrowded interior is typical of the Victorian era. In the eyes of Modernist architects, such an accumulation of furniture and objects would call for drastic cleaning. Its purpose would be not only to get rid of ornamental superfluousness, but also to drive away the ghosts that haunt it.

Besides the living, another type of subject appears at this stage: the departed for whom ornament may be interpreted as a kind of offering.

The role of ornament vis-à-vis the dead is present from the start in the Vitruvian tradition, through the famous story regarding the invention of the Corinthian capital by Greek sculptor Callimachus. The story recounted by Vitruvius in his *Ten Books on Architecture* links the living to the dead, ornament to offering, the fecundity of nature to the creative power of the artist:

> It is related that the original discovery of this form of capital was as follows. A freeborn maiden of Corinth, just of marriageable age, was attacked by an illness and passed away. After her burial, her nurse, collecting a few things which used to give the girl pleasure while she was alive, put them in a basket, carried it to the tomb, and laid it on top thereof, covering it with a roof-tile so that the things might last longer in the open air. This basket happened to be placed just above the root of an acanthus. The acanthus root, pressed down meanwhile though it was by the weight, when springtime came round put forth leaves and stalks in the middle, and the stalks, growing up along the

Dennis Maher, Fargo House, Room for the Image and the Reflected Image, Buffalo, New York, 2010– .
A contemporary artistic project, the ornamental dimension of which claims the heritage of Soane's or Loti's houses. In tune with our post-industrial and environmentally oriented society, recycling is now allied with accumulation and collage.

sides of the basket, and pressed out by the corners of the tile through the compulsion of its weight, were forced to bend into volutes at the outer edges.

Just then Callimachus (…) passed by this tomb and observed the basket with the tender young leaves growing round it. Delighted with the novel style and form, he built some columns after that pattern for the Corinthians, determined their symmetrical proportions, and established from that time forth the rules to be followed in finished works of the Corinthian order.[36]

Towards the end of the 17th century, the first director and professor of the French Academy of Architecture François Blondel (not to be confused with his 18th-century homonym, Jacques-François) clearly had this story in mind when he imagined that the origin of the capitals was more generally to be found in the early Greek custom of placing the urns containing the ashes of the deceased on top of columns.[37]

Ornament is not only meant to adorn life; it also commemorates the dead. This role can be grasped immediately when one walks into a traditional cemetery with its decorated graves. Interestingly, the Modernist ban on ornamentation never really applied to the dead. Furthermore, undertakers have remained faithful to this day to a conception of ornament as social marker. From the ornamental fixtures of the casket to the engravings and sculptures of the tombstone, everything in their world has a price and implication in terms of social prestige.

Industrialisation and the Ornamental Impulse

The 19th century marks both the triumph of ornament and the beginning of the crisis that will lead to its critique and rejection by Modernism. Throughout the century, ornaments accumulate almost everywhere, from handmade objects and industrial products to furniture and buildings. Bourgeois interiors revel in the clutter of bibelots, while urban public spaces are filled with monuments and statues. The various 'grammars' of ornament published at the time appear as a direct consequence of this proliferation, and also as a symptom of the unease generated by the issues it raises, beginning with the difficulty to master it.[38] British architect and artist Owen Jones, the author of the most famous of these publications, unintentionally reveals the extent of the problem with his 'General principles in the arrangement of form and colour in architecture and the decorative arts', which try to assign rules to

L'Origine des Chapiteaux des Colonnes.

the decorative sprawl. 'Construction should be decorated. Decoration should never be purposely constructed,' writes Jones in complete contradiction to the way many ornaments described in his grammar actually function. He continues: 'Beauty of form is produced by lines growing out one from the other in gradual undulations: there are no excrescences; nothing could be removed and leave the design equally good or better.'[39] There again, excrescences are not absent from Jones's grammar, far from it.

Ornamental profusion of the 19th century is largely attributable to industrialisation. As we have seen, industrialisation made possible the prefabrication of an ever-increasing number of ornaments. Above all, its productions offered new domains of application to the ornamental arts. Manufacturers adorned machines as well as all sorts of factory-made goods like electroplate wares, despite Ruskin's reservations about the attempt to reconcile industrial utility and genuine human pleasure. These reservations had led him to his famous ban on the use of decoration in railway stations.[40] The richly ornamented cast-iron stoves and other useful appliances displayed in universal exhibitions of the second half of the century would have appeared even more abhorrent to his eyes had he deigned to reflect upon them.[41]

In parallel with this generalisation of ornamental practices, historicism, one of the dominant features of the century, revealed their enduring character as well as the diversity of the ornaments invented by the various civilisations ancient to modern. Following a rapid evocation of 'Ornament of Savage Tribes', Jones's grammar reviews for instance Egyptian, Assyrian, Greek, Pompeian, Roman, Byzantine, Arabian, Turkish, Moresque, Persian, Indian, Hindoo, Chinese and Celtic ornaments. Then comes the series of Western European ornaments from the medieval and Renaissance periods

Owen Jones, 'Egyptian', from *The Grammar of Ornament*, 1868.
In addition to the diversity of historic styles, polychromy represents another fundamental realisation of the 19th century regarding architectural décor. A pioneer of modern colour theory, Owen Jones was responsible for the colour scheme adopted for the Great Exhibition building of 1851, Joseph Paxton's Crystal Palace.

AEGYPTISCH EGYPTIAN N°3 EGYPTIENS
TAFEL. VI PL. VI

on, and from Italy to England. Other authors may have divided their material differently, but they all shared the same fascination for the universality of ornament as a human phenomenon and for the variety of forms that it has taken both historically and geographically.

Approached in these terms, ornament appears both as the outcome of a fundamental human impulse, which Piranesi had announced with his unbridled taste for decorative accumulation, and as a mirror reflecting the specificity of the culture that has produced it. British historian of art Ralph Wornum evoked 'a natural propensity to decorate or embellish whatever is useful or agreeable to us', modulated by civilisation and taste and 'essential in commercial prosperity', a factor that explains its importance for industrialists and merchants.[42] In a given society, a common inspiration seems at work in the various domains where the ornamental impulse expresses itself. This inspiration enabled Gottfried Semper to relate the capitals designed by the Egyptians and the hairstyles of their women.[43] Limited to architecture, such kinship between the diverse elements that adorn buildings represents a key aspect of style. Indeed, architectural styles involve, of course, tectonic solutions such as trabeation for Greek or the lancet arch and ribbed vault for Gothic; but they are as much about the ornaments used and the relation they have with one another.

Gottfried Semper's monumental attempt to provide new theoretical ground for architecture is representative of the progressive shift of the question of ornamentation towards an anthropological footing that would mark debates in the last decades of the century. Indeed, if ornamentation is rooted in a deep human impulse, how is it to be engaged independently from a set of very general issues regarding man and society? By the same token, the

Owen Jones, 'Illuminated MSS', from *The Grammar of Ornament*, 1868.
In Owen Jones's *Grammar*, architectural ornament proves inseparable from other types of adornment, such as manuscript illuminations illustrated here. This led him to show an interest in all sorts of flat patterns, an interest that resonates with contemporary designers.

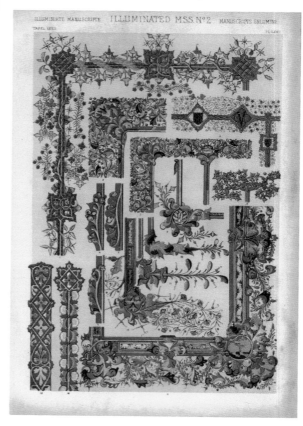

Model of a beam steam engine, circa 1840.
This single-cylinder engine was typically in use in small workshops and businesses. Its frame is shaped in the form of a Classical colonnade as if to soften the contrast between the realm of the arts and humanities and the rising world of technology. Quite common at the time, the attempt to classicise the machine is also inseparable from the quest for a genuine industrial aesthetic.

various subjects of ornament tend to merge into a generic human being who produces and makes use of decoration in an almost instinctive way.

The ornamental impulse seems to be rooted in the very rhythms of life. This connection is especially evident in 19th-century German culture. As American historian of science Norton Wise has shown, while German neo-Classical artists had explored repeatedly the expressive and decorative power of the line during the first decades of the century, younger physicists of the second half of the century, such as Hermann Helmholtz or Emil du Bois-Reymond, were fascinated by the power of curves to retranscribe the fundamental mechanism of organic life, like the excitation of nerves and the contraction of muscles.[44] Lines and curves thus appear from the arts to the study of living beings and may be interpreted as a common thread relating the ornamental regime to the living activity that constitutes its substrates, as if the hand that draws were actually emulating more fundamental rhythms of organic life. Such a conviction is admirably conveyed by the extraordinary composition drawn by Emil du Bois-Reymond for the membership certificate of the Berlin

Cast-iron stoves on display
at the Chicago Columbian
Exposition, 1893.
These decorated stoves
are emblematic of the
alliance between industrial
production and ornament.
Contrary to the other
patterns and figures, the
urns at the top have a partly
functional purpose: they
allow water to evaporate in
order to humidify the hot
dry air.

Physical Society. In this highly decorative drawing, scientific practice rises like
a tree from a labyrinthine series of lines that appears in turn as a rhizomatic
root structure and as a complex signature.

Results of the ornamental impulse can be observed almost everywhere and
in all sorts of situations. Body tattoos are ornamental, just like the cast-
iron Doric columns that often adorn 19th-century steam-engine frames.
Tattoos fascinate the authors that try to grapple with ornament. A Maori
tattooed head is among the most famous illustrations of Jones's *Grammar
of Ornament*. 'Man's earliest ambition is to create. To this feeling must be
ascribed the tattooing of the human face and body,' writes the architect
before adding that such practice is typical of the savage trying 'to increase
the expression by which he seeks to strike terror in his enemies or rivals, or to
create what appears to him as a new beauty'.[45]

During the second half of the 19th century, ornament became even more
ambiguous than before because of this untamed, almost savage connotation,
which Ruskin had already pinpointed without drawing all the possible
conclusions from it. Indeed, an excessive fondness for adornment seems to
point towards a primitive, almost barbaric level of psychological development.

Gottfried Semper,
Eygptian capital and
ladies' hair decoration,
from *Style in the Technical
and Tectonic Arts; or,
Practical Aesthetics*,
1860–63.
According to Semper, there
is a direct and evident
connection between
sculpture, architecture and
costume. In the case of the
Egyptians, the use of lotus
flowers for column capitals
derived in his eyes from
the way ladies ornamented
their heads by attaching
stalks of these flowers. This
hypothesis is not far from
the traditional interpretation
of the Ionic capital as a
transposition of Ionian
women's hairstyle.

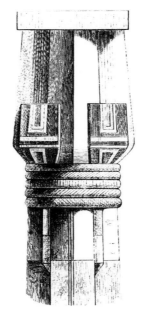

Gottfried Semper,
plaiting, from *Style
in the Technical and
Tectonic Arts; or, Practical
Aesthetics*, 1860–63.
One of the most famous
aspects of Gottfried
Semper's theory is the
importance given to textile
in the origins and early
developments of applied arts
and architecture. Through
actions like knotting and
plaiting, textile enables us to
understand how elementary
gestures condition the
emergence of decorative
patterns.

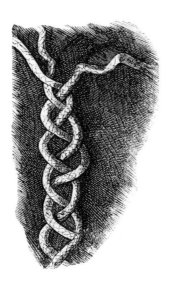

And since bourgeois ideology tends to interpret the criminal mind as primitive and childish, the conditions are gradually met to assimilate overindulgence in ornament to a sort of crime against higher human values: what happens when one lets the brutal forces of life overwhelm the fragile construction of civilisation and reason. Following bourgeois stereotypes again, ornament is also more female than male, since to the positivist mind the female constitution seems less prone to reason than its male counterpart.

One cannot but continue to be struck by the way such interpretations echo some of the preoccupations that gave birth to psychoanalysis: the fear of the wild and untamed mental forces that loom under the varnish of education, and the desire to find a way to cure the excesses to which they lead. Since it seems to be plugged into such anthropological and mental depths, ornament gradually transforms itself into a highly problematic manifestation of civilisation. Its multiplication may be construed as a mark of progress, because of its links with industrialisation, but it also runs the risk of a return to the dark forces of irrationality. Italian criminologist Cesare Lombroso made this latter aspect evident. Linking criminal disposition to primitiveness, he reviewed the ornamental practices of criminals from tattoos to graffiti. Tattoos take on a special importance in his eyes as the markers of primitive and criminally oriented subjects. The lesson will not be lost on Loos who proves even more assertive in 'Ornament and Crime':

'The modern person who tattoos himself is either a criminal or a degenerate,' he wrote. 'There are prisons in which eighty percent of the inmates have tattoos. People with tattoos not in prison are either latent criminals or degenerate aristocrats.'[46]

As Andrew Herscher and Jimena Canales have convincingly argued, 'Ornament and Crime' must thus be understood in a much more literal way.[47] At the dawn of Modernism, ornament, because of its deep anthropological and social resonances, not only carried with it the risks of bad taste and dissolution of tectonic codes. It could also be seen as a stigma on any individual who indulged in it. As Herscher and Canales note, 'Loos infantilized, orientalized, feminized and criminalized specific Austrian and German architects and designers who employed ornament.'[48] The Modernist ban on traditional architectural décor amounts to a condemnation passed on certain types of subjects.

The Ghost of Ornament

Owen Jones, female head from New Zealand, from *The Grammar of Ornament*, 1868. According to Jones, body tattoos represent one of the first expressions of the ornamental impulse. The stamping of patterns on the covering of the body, either skin or cloth, comes next. In body tattoos, beauty meets with the desire to inspire awe.

Despite Loos's adamant statements on its lack of relevance, ornament never disappeared entirely from architecture. Of course, Modernism wiped statues, mascarons and even cornices from building facades. It cleaned interiors even more drastically, so that the crude light of electricity would illuminate immaculate rooms. But the ornamental dimension remained present under different guises. Tectonic articulations could reveal themselves to be ornamental just like dramatic spatial effects. In addition, as Alina Payne has shown, many of the everyday objects designed by early Modernist architects, from furniture to houseware, were imparted with an expressive function formerly devoted to architectural ornament.[49]

Later in the 20th century, other modes of alternative ornamental practices developed, such as the use of concrete formwork traces by Le Corbusier. From the 1950s on, the rediscovery of proportions by various Modernist architects influenced by Rudolf Wittkower's *Architectural Principles in the Age of Humanism*, as well as by the cybernetic approach of the relations

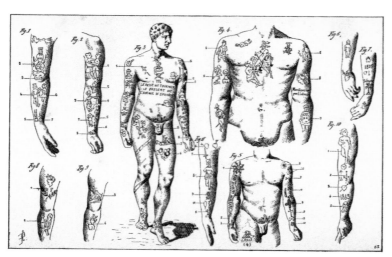

between man and his environment, led to new research in rhythm and modulation imbued with decorative potential. With his Modulor, Le Corbusier appears there again as a key figure.[50] Around the same time, the exploration of patterns by artists and architects ranging from György Kepes to Eero Saarinen also began to develop.[51] At the intersection of organisational and expressive concerns, these early uses of pattern can also be subsumed under the category of the ornamental.

From the immersive character of certain spatial effects to the role played by materiality and patterns, many aspects of the contemporary return of ornament can thus be related to earlier Modernist experiments. The importance gleaned by the notion of affect is also rooted in the Modernist quest for a certain pervasiveness of the ornamental. Nevertheless, explicit ornamentation was rigorously contained. Owen Jones's recommendation that construction should be decorated and that decoration should never be purposely constructed was finally applied.

In Modernist architecture, the status of ornament evokes the fate of Lewis Carroll's famous Cheshire cat grin, which floats some time in the air after the disappearance of the

Richard Neutra Listens to a Client, *Time*, 15 August 1949.
In his attempt to steer Modernism away from the risk of anonymity, Richard Neutra thought of himself as a kind of psychoanalyst in charge of the production of highly personal and affective environments.

NEUTRA LISTENS TO A CLIENT

face. The ghost of a smile, all that is left of a visage: such fate brings us back to the most profound consequence of the ban on traditional architectural décor. With the demise of any explicit ornamental vocabulary, the very presence of the various subjects of architecture changed dramatically. The architect remained physically present in his creation, but without a discernible face. The worker disappeared almost entirely. As for the client, the great temptation was to reduce him to a mere user, that is, a body for which needs play the role traditionally devoted to physiognomy. Of course, Modernism tried constantly to find antidotes to such reduction. Richard Neutra's understanding of the architect as a kind of psychoanalyst addressing the hidden desires of his client is one instance among many others of the project to reestablish a fully-fledged subject of architecture.[52] Yet the risk of anonymity continued to loom.

References

1 For a very similar type of reflection on this issue, see Laurent Baridon, Martial Guédron, *Corps et Arts: Physionomies et Physiologies dans les Arts Visuels* (Paris: L'Harmattan, 1999), pp 189–228.
2 Françoise Choay, *The Rule and the Model: On the Theory of Architecture and Urbanism* (Paris, 1980, English trs, Cambridge, MA: MIT Press, 1997).
3 See Nigel Llewellyn, 'Two Notes on Diego da Sagredo', *Journal of the Warburg and Courtauld Institutes*, vol 40, 1977, pp 292–300.
4 Jacques-François Blondel, *Cours d'Architecture* (Paris: Desaint, 1771–7), t 1, pl X–XII.
5 John W Nunley, Cara McCarty (eds), *Masks: Faces of Culture* (St Louis, MO: St Louis Art Museum, 1999), 'Introduction', pp 15–17, p 17 in particular.
6 Peter Sloterdijk, *Bubbles: Spheres Volume I: Microspherology* (Frankfurt, 1998, English trs, Los Angeles: Semiotext(e), 2011).
7 Cf Wolfgang Herrmann, *The Theory of Claude Perrault* (London: Zwemmer, 1973); Antoine Picon, *Claude Perrault 1613–1688 ou la*

Curiosité d'un Classique (Paris: Picard, 1988).
8 Sebastiano Serlio, *Book IV*, 1537, quoted in Alina A Payne, *The Architectural Treatise in the Italian Renaissance: Architectural Invention, Ornament, and Literary Culture* (Cambridge: Cambridge University Press, 1999), p 15.
9 Payne, *The Architectural Treatise in the Italian Renaissance*, pp 116–22. In addition to Payne's book, regarding the issue of licence and invention in Serlio's work, see Mario Carpo, *La Maschera e il Modello: Teoria architettonica ed Evangelismo nell'Extraordinario Libro di Sebastiano Serlio* (Milan: Jaca Book, 1993).
10 On Delorme's overall conception of invention, see Robin Evans, *The Projective Cast: Architecture and its Three Geometries* (Cambridge, MA: MIT Press, 1995), pp 180–9, and above all Philippe Potié, *Philibert De L'Orme: Figures de la Pensée Constructive* (Marseilles: Parenthèses, 1996). Both authors focus mainly on the constructive aspect of Philibert Delorme's work. In the eyes of

Delorme, there is, however, a profound continuity between constructive and ornamental invention.
11 Potié, *Philibert De L'Orme*, p 45.
12 Etienne-Louis Boullée, *Architecture. Essai sur l'Art* (Paris: Hermann, 1968), p 61.
13 Giovanni Battista Piranesi, *Observations on the Letter of Monsieur Mariette with Opinions on Architecture, and a Preface to a New Treatise on the Introduction and Progress of the Fine Arts in Europe in Ancient Times* (Rome, 1765, English trs Los Angeles: Getty Research Institute, 2002), p 98. For a detailed analysis of Piranesi's position, see John Wilton-Ely's introduction to Piranesi's translation. See also William Reader, 'Piranesi's Diverse Maniere', *The Burlington Magazine*, vol 115, no 842, May 1973, pp 308–17; Erika Naginski, 'Preliminary Thoughts on Piranesi and Vico', *Res. Anthropology and Aesthetics,* no 53/54; Spring/Fall 2008, pp 150–65.
14 Manfredo Tafuri, *The Sphere and the Labyrinth: Avant-Gardes and Architecture from Piranesi to the 1970s* (Turin, 1980,

English trs Cambridge, MA, 1987), pp 25–40 in particular.
15 On this impulsive dimension, see Didier Laroque, *Le Discours de Piranèse: L'Ornement Sublime et le Suspens de l'Architecture* (Paris: Les Editions de la Passion, 1999), pp 117–47.
16 Tafuri, *The Sphere and the Labyrinth*.
17 Frank Lloyd Wright, 'Louis H Sullivan – His Work', *Architectural Record*, 56/1, July 1924, pp 28–32, p 29 in particular, quoted in David Van Zanten, *Sullivan's City: The Meaning of Ornament for Louis Sullivan* (New York, London: WW Norton & Company, 2000), p 1.
18 See on this question K Michael Hays, *Modernism and the Posthumanist Subject: The Architecture of Hannes Meyer and Ludwig Hilberseimer* (Cambridge, MA: MIT Press, 1992). On the importance of the body of the architect in the practice of architecture, we are also indebted to Michel Baridon, 'Le Mythe de Dinocrate: L'Architecture, le Corps et l'Utopie', manuscript submitted for the Habilitation à Diriger des Recherches at Université de Paris I Panthéon-Sorbonne,

2005.
19 Katie Scott, *The Rococo Interior: Decoration and Social Spaces in Early Eighteenth-Century Paris* (New Haven, London: Yale University Press, 1995), p 7.
20 Cf Potié, *Philibert De L'Orme*.
21 Augustin-Charles d'Aviler, *Cours d'Architecture* (Paris: Nicolas Langlois, 1691), pl A.
22 Renaud d'Enfert, *L'Enseignement du Dessin en France: Figure Humaine et Dessin Géométrique (1750–1850)* (Paris: Belin, 2003).
23 Valérie Nègre, *L'Ornement en Série: Architecture, Terre Cuite et Carton-Pierre* (Sprimont: Mardaga, 2006).
24 Reyner Banham, *Theory and Design in the First Machine Age* (New York: Praeger, 1960); Kenneth Frampton, *Modern Architecture: A Critical History* (London: Thames & Hudson, 1980).
25 Martin Bressani, 'Science, Histoire et Archéologie: Sources et Généalogie de la Pensée Organiciste de Viollet-le-Duc', PhD dissertation submitted at Université de Paris IV Sorbonne, 1997.
26 Auguste Choisy, *L'Art de*

Bâtir chez les Byzantins (Paris: Librairie de la Société Anonyme de Publications Périodiques, 1883), p 170.
27 Cf d'Enfert, *L'Enseignement du Dessin en France;* Arindam Dutta, *The Bureaucracy of Beauty: Design in the Age of its Global Reproductibility* (New York: Taylor & Francis, 2007).
28 Eve Blau, *Ruskinian Gothic: The Architecture of Deane and Woodward, 1845–1861* (Princeton: Princeton University Press, 1982).
29 Jacques-Bénigne Bossuet, *Introduction à la Philosophie, ou de la Connaissance de Dieu, et de Soi-Mesme* (Paris: R.-M. d'Espilly, 1722), pp 37–8.
30 Quoted by Scott, *The Rococo Interior*, p 83.
31 Charles Perrault, *Pensées Chrétiennes* (Paris, Seattle, Tübingen: Biblio 17, 1987), p 108.
32 On the myths and realities of the boudoir, see Ed Lilley, 'The Name of the Boudoir', *The Journal of the Society of Architectural Historians*, vol 53, no 2, June 1994, pp 193–8.
33 Cf Monique Eleb, Anne Debarre, *Architectures de*

la Vie Privée, Maisons et Mentalités XVIIe–XIXe siècles, (Brussels: Archives d'Architecture Moderne, 1989).

34 Walter Benjamin, 'Paris, the Capital of the Nineteenth Century', 1935, published in Walter Benjamin, *Selected Writings*, vol 3, 1935–8 (Cambridge, MA, London: Harvard University Press, 2002), pp 32–49, p 39 in particular.

35 See, for instance, Helen Dorey, '12–14 Lincoln's Inn Fields', in Margaret Richardson, MaryAnne Stevens (eds), *John Soane Architect: Master of Space and Light* (London: Royal Academy of Arts, 1999), pp 150–73.

36 Vitruvius, *The Ten Books on Architecture*, translated by Morris H Morgan (Cambridge, MA: Harvard University Press, 1914), pp 104–6.

37 François Blondel, *Cours d'architecture* (Paris: P Aubouin, F Clouzier, 1675–83), Part II, pp 2–3.

38 See on this theme Rémi Labrusse, 'Face au Chaos: Grammaires de l'Ornement', *Perspective: La Revue de l'INHA*, 2010–11, 1, pp 97–121.

39 Owen Jones, *The Grammar of Ornament* (London, 1856, new edition London: Bernard Quaritch, 1868), p 5.

40 John Ruskin, *The Seven Lamps of Architecture* (New York: John Wiley, 1849), p 100 in particular.

41 Cf Julie Wosk, *Breaking Frame: Technology and the Visual Arts in the Nineteenth Century* (New Brunswick, NJ: Rutgers University Press, 1992).

42 Ralph N Wornum, *Analysis of Ornament, Characteristics of Style: An Introduction to the Study of the History of Ornamental Art* (London: Chapman & Hall, 1896), p 3.

43 Gottfried Semper, *Style in the Technical and Tectonic Arts; or, Practical Aesthetics* (Frankfurt, Munich, 1860–63, English trs, Los Angeles: Getty Research Institute, 2004), p 238.

44 Norton Wise, *Neo-Classical Aesthetics of Art and Science: Hermann Helmholtz and the Frog-Drawing Machine*, The Hans Rausing Lecture 2007 (Uppsala: Uppsala University, 2008); Norton Wise, 'What's in a Line?', in Moritz Epple, Claus Zittel (eds), *Science as Cultural Practice. Vol 1: Cultures and Politics of Research from the Early Modern Period to the Age of Extremes* (Berlin: Akademie Verlag, 2010), pp 61–102.

45 Jones, *The Grammar of Ornament*, p 13.

46 Adolf Loos, 'Ornament and Crime', 1929, republished in Adolf Loos, *Ornament and Crime: Selected Essays* (Riverside, California, Ariadne Press, 1998), p 167.

47 Jimena Canales and Andrew Herscher, 'Tattoos and Modern Architecture in the Work of Adolf Loos', *Architectural History*, vol 48, 2005, pp 235–56.

48 *Ibid*, p 237.

49 Alina Payne, *From Ornament to Object: Genealogies of Architectural Modernism* (New Haven, London: Yale University Press, 2012).

50 Christopher Hight, *Architectural Principles in the Age of Cybernetics* (New York: Routledge, 2008).

51 Reinhold Martin, *The Organizational Complex: Architecture, Media, and Corporate Space* (Cambridge, MA: MIT Press, 2003).

52 Cf Sylvia Lavin, *Form Follows Libido: Architecture and Richard Neutra in a Psychoanalytic Culture* (Cambridge, MA: MIT Press, 2004).

3

Politics of Ornament

Today, architectural ornament is often approached in qualitative terms. Scholars, historians of art in particular, will readily interpret it as one of the most emblematic expressions of the pursuit of pleasure and beauty, which is supposed to characterise all sorts of artistic endeavour, including architecture.[1] By contrast, contemporary digital designers are hesitant about the use of an ostensibly loaded term like beauty, preferring to evoke the production of affects ornament allows. In both cases, qualitative rather than quantitative issues seem at stake. Such was not always the case. Until the dawn of Modernism, quantitative approaches played an essential role: ornament was an economic problem as much as an aesthetic one. Politics rests partly on the management of wealth. In order to understand the relationship between ornamentation and politics, it is worth evoking the traditional economics of ornament. It offers precious insight into the political relevance of architectural décor.

From Economics to Politics

The fundamental factor lies in the cost of ornament. Décor matters in an almost literal sense because of the amount of material and degree of labour involved in its production. Until Modernism, material and labour gave a special importance to the quantity survey of architectural ornament. In the case of 17th- and 18th-century France, the proper way to account for the stone used to create mouldings constituted, for instance, a key issue for the professionals of architecture and construction. Specialist of survey techniques Pierre Bullet devoted pages of his widely circulated treatise, *L'Architecture Pratique* (Practical Architecture), to this question.[2] Published initially in 1691, Bullet's overview of quantity survey remained in use for over a century. It provided practitioners with convenient ways to measure all the parts of a building, including its ornaments.

Beyond this kind of technical issue, ornament represents an investment. Properly managed, it can accrue and constitute a kind of heirloom, like jewels that literally are worth their weight in precious metals. The Ancient Roman approach to the question of ornamentation bore the mark of such consideration. According to Roman law, ornament corresponded to a category of properties that were neither immovable like houses, nor completely mobile like furniture. Occupying a middle ground between these two extremes, they were fixed but proved removable if necessary. Revealingly, a Senatus Consultum passed in the year AD 44 forbade selling the ornaments of a house, a measure that targeted Patrician families in particular. In the eyes of the Roman legislator, ornament appeared almost literally as a capital, a patrimony, that was supposed to increase instead of being dispersed.[3] The same conception applied at the scale of the city: to adorn it was synonymous with a process of accumulation. In Rome one could admire ornaments in almost every public space, from the Capitol to the various Imperial Fora. Either brought from distant provinces or produced by local artists and artisans, they appeared as a treasure exposed to the eyes of the multitude. For the Romans, ornament represented a quantitative as much as a qualitative issue.

Pierre Bullet, frontispiece of *L'Architecture Pratique*, 1691.
The frontispiece of this highly successful French treatise on quantitative survey shows a man measuring a column while others discuss the merit of the building. Quantitative survey is the natural auxiliary of theory. Without it, ornaments cannot be fully appreciated.

Sumptuary laws constituted another crucial expression of this quantitative approach to ornament since part of their justification lay in the prohibition of unnecessary expenses that could ruin families and ultimately the state. From

Forum of Nerva, Rome,
AD 97.
Built by Emperor Domitian,
the forum was inaugurated
by his successor, Nerva, who
gave it its name. The marbles
function as ornaments at the
scale of the city.

Venice to England, and from France to the Netherlands, almost every early modern European nation passed such laws. They forbade overly luxurious clothes and more generally any purportedly improper use of ornament. For instance, a 17th-century Venetian law banned the painting of gondolas in order to avoid the extravagant decorations in which the rich tended to indulge. This is why they have remained black to this day. Moderate consumption was deemed good, while excessive consumption could bring only doom on houses, cities and nations.

Sumptuary laws were aimed at maintaining social hierarchy, or rather the correspondence between the various social ranks and the visual markers that were supposed to apply to them. From clothes to buildings, inappropriate ornament could disrupt this correspondence, thus endangering the hierarchy, legibility and very structure of society. What would happen to the pyramid of orders and conditions instituted by God and maintained by kings and bishops, if the bourgeois began to dress as aristocrats, and bankers lived behind facades suited to the residences of dukes and princes? Sumptuary laws were about money, but also about visible signs of distinction. The ornaments targeted by their clauses involved these two aspects. To be more accurate, these ornaments appeared as operators, which could transform money into signs, capital into social distinction. In other words, they made possible the passage from quantity to quality, from the cost of materials and labour to visual and social communication.

From the Roman obsession with accruing a quantity of ornaments to the sumptuary laws passed to limit their use in early modern Europe, the various forms taken by the economics of ornament ultimately revolved around three dimensions: wealth, legal prescriptions and social communication. These dimensions appear as fundamental components of politics. Traditional ornament was imbued with political meaning because it involved capital, customs and/or laws, and above all social communication.

Communication and Style

From the Renaissance to the beginning of the 20th century, the politics of ornament generally focused on communication. In addition to pleasing the eye, ornament was supposed to provide decisive information on the nature of the building it adorned as well as on the importance and rank of the institution it hosted and/or the owner who had paid for it. Information

Robert Smirke, British Museum, London, 1823–46.
Deeply moved by Greek temples that he saw during his Grand Tour, architect Robert Smirke based the capitals of his Ionic order for the British Museum on those of the temple of Athena Polias at Priene. The Ionic order had already been used for a museum by Leo von Klenze for the Munich Glyptothek. For 19th-century architects, museums were temples dedicated to culture in a very literal sense.

began with the five orders themselves, which were associated with degrees of slenderness and refinement as well as with certain types of programmes and patrons. Whereas the Tuscan order presented a sturdy and utilitarian connotation well suited to city gates and military buildings, the Doric order fitted constructions of a more dignified nature. Doric constructions could still

William Welles Bosworth, AT&T Building, New York, 1916.
A remarkable combination of Doric and Ionic is meant to convey the cultural importance of the telegraph and telephone. The message was reinforced by the lobby of the building, which evoked the inner chamber of a Doric temple. The architect later referred to the building as his 'temple on Broadway'.

possess a utilitarian character, but they could also serve higher civic or religious purposes as with temples. The Ionic went ordinarily with another level of refinement to be found, for instance, in buildings devoted to the cultivation of the arts. With the Corinthian, magnificence vied with elegance; a combination especially fit for royal mansions. With its slender proportions, the Composite order emphasised the predominance of décor over structural logic. It was especially adapted to the adornment of triumphal arches or theatres.[4]

These general guidelines were complicated by the practice of superimposed orders that enabled architects to put slender orders on more solid ones, Ionic on Doric, Corinthian on Ionic, and Composite on Corinthian. There again, symbolic and programmatic conventions applied to these combinations. To enrich them further, Claude Perrault tried to invent a French order, even lighter than the Composite, at the end of the 17th century. To express this lightness, Perrault proposed to replace the acanthus leaves with ostrich feathers on the capital of the new type of column.[5] However, the idea was short-lived and the five Classical orders maintained their quasi monopoly.

The orders enabled architects to elaborate a remarkably rich and complex discourse with their clients, both individual and institutional. This discourse would stay in use throughout the 19th and well into the 20th centuries. Many museums remained, for example, faithful to the use of the Ionic order, beginning with Robert Smirke's British Museum in London (1823–46), or Karl Friedrich Schinkel's Altes Museum in Berlin (1830).[6] The same order was also considered as well adapted to institutions of higher learning. Like McKim, Mead & White at Columbia University, architect William Welles Bosworth employed the Ionic for the Massachusetts Institute of Technology's new campus in Cambridge (1916).[7]

The message conveyed by the choice of orders proved sometimes even more elaborate, especially after the rise of historicism, which accustomed architects to a new level of sophistication in the manipulation of styles. When Bosworth used a Doric order for the first floor of his AT&T building in New York (1916),

McKim, Meade & White,
Pennsylvania Station, New
York, 1910.
The waiting room and its
Corinthian order evoked
Imperial Rome, more
specifically the Baths of
Caracalla. Through its décor,
19th- and early 20th-century
architecture evoked remote
places and time. Ornament
was always to a certain
extent haunted by episodes
from the past. Architectural
expression dwelt on absence
as much as presence.

he suggested a complex set of meanings. They ranged from the nature of the
service provided by the telegraph and telephone company to the notion that
modern communication possessed a spiritual dimension, since the Doric order
could be used both for utilitarian constructions and for temples and churches.
In the superior floors of the AT&T building, the Ionic replaced the Doric,
which should not come as a surprise, since the Doric had prepared the viewer
to recognise the cultural dimension of the telegraph and telephone.

McKim, Mead & White's reference to the Baths of Caracalla at their
Pennsylvania Station in New York (1910) revealed itself equally intelligent.[8]
The main waiting room emulated its Roman model not only because of its
gigantic scale. The Corinthian order chosen by the architects also possessed
an imperial aspect. The political relevance of such a choice for what was
probably the most remarkable North American Beaux-Arts railway station
ever built appeared evident to their contemporaries. Just like Roman baths,

modern stations hosted large crowds. The imperial connotation was especially well suited to a construction located in the heart of the 'Empire State', the motto of New York. An imperial architecture for a democratic empire: the message could not be clearer.

As elaborate as they could reveal themselves to be, especially at the climax of historicism when the manipulation of ornaments borrowed from the past reached a new level of virtuosity, the indications offered by the orders provided only general orientations. They constituted a kind of canvas on which the architect was supposed to lay the detail of his décor like strokes of colours, in accordance with the position occupied by his client in the social hierarchy. In addition to the information conveyed by the order chosen for the facades and the degree of richness of the décor, architectural ornaments could communicate more specifically through symbolic elements, like coats of arms for palaces and aristocratic hotels, and trophies for military buildings. Architectural décor was supposed to stabilise society by mirroring its structure and permanence.

Madruzzo coat of arms above the balcony of Palazzo Roccabruna, Trento, Italy, 16th century. With this type of ornament, the relation between architectural décor and social rank is especially conspicuous.

This function was fundamentally political, since it reinforced the chains of command and obedience that framed the relations between groups and individuals. Ornaments supported position and social rank. They played an important role in the ephemeral décors built for the various ceremonies, which asserted the legitimacy of the reigning powers, from the Royal Entries into cities to princes' and princesses' weddings and funerals.[9] Moments of crisis like the fall out of favour of Louis XIV's Superintendent of Finances, Nicolas Fouquet in August 1661, made this role even more conspicuous. The minister's disgrace was hastened by his improper use of ornaments in the castle and gardens of Vaux-le-Vicomte (1661). His estate possessed something royal, not so much because of its size but rather because of the magnificence of its architectural décor. The impropriety was aggravated by the lavish banquet and spectacle offered to the King upon his visit. Revealingly, Louis XIV hired the entire team of artists responsible for the creation of Vaux-le-Vicomte to

John Talman, Military trophy, 17th–18th century. Military trophies like this one were extremely common throughout the early modern period. They reign for instance on the top of the West facade of Versailles as well as on the facades and roofs of many other royal and aristocratic residences.

work at Versailles: architect Louis Le Vau, landscape architect André Le Nôtre, painter Charles Le Brun, among them. Their subsequent task would be to transform what was still a modest royal hunting lodge into something even more impressive than Fouquet's estate. At Versailles, the political message conveyed by the ornaments would reach a new level of coherence through themes borrowed from Greco-Roman mythology as well as through a bellicose vocabulary extolling the military victories of the Sun King.[10]

Versailles achieved the transposition to secular power of a practice that the Church had already perfected on a grand scale before and after the Counter Reformation. Despite the major changes brought by the Council of Trent during the second half of the 16th century, Catholicism remained faithful to the belief that décor represented a powerful means of spiritual government. At an intermediary scale between building and sculpture, St Peter's baldachin (1634) was nothing if not a giant ornament. Interestingly, with its impressive mass of bronze, Bernini's creation remained faithful to the quantitative dimension that had characterised Ancient Roman *ornamenta*.

Until the dawn of industrialisation, the politics of architectural ornamentation remained relatively straightforward for two reasons. The first lay in the limited number of admissible ornaments in a tradition dominated by Greco-Roman references. Despite the inventiveness of Renaissance and Baroque

Veue et perspectiue du Chasteau de Vaux le Vicomte du costé de l'entrée

au coin des Mathurins   Chez Nicolas Poilly rüe St Jacques a la belle Image auec priuil. du Roy   1 S

architects and artists, most decorative elements followed established patterns. A second reason had to do with the very nature of politics in societies of the Ancien Régime. Even if popes and bishops, kings and princes often followed divergent agendas, if families and clans intrigued and fought bitterly for distinctions and riches, power games rarely challenged the predominant vision of society as a pyramid of conditions. Under these conditions, political communication consisted in representing the legitimacy and magnificence of the established powers and expressing as accurately as possible the various ranks of the institutions and individuals subjected to their authority.[11] Whereas disagreement could arise over the degree of lavishness suitable for an elevated position or over the exact rank of a family or an individual, the need for an overall hierarchy and the general features it should possess were seldom questioned.

During the second half of the 18th century, the discovery of the diversity of architectures that had developed in countries ranging from Egypt to China began to undermine this stable frame of reference. The progressive opening

Vaux-le-Vicomte, anonymous engraving showing the entrance, 17th century. Purchased by Nicolas Fouquet in 1641, the estate of Vaux-le-Vicomte was transformed by Louis XIV's superintendent of finances into a lavish residence. The castle itself was rebuilt by Louis Le Vau, while André Le Nôtre designed the gardens. Poet Jean de La Fontaine and playwright Molière, two protégés of Nicolas Fouquet, were regular guests at Vaux-le-Vicomte.

Jean-Baptiste Massé, allegory of the war against Spain for the rights of the Queen, engraving after a painting by Charles Le Brun on the ceiling of the Hall of Mirrors in Versailles, 18th century.

A war was waged against Spain in 1667 to defend the succession rights of Queen Marie-Thérèse, Louis XIV's spouse. On the ceiling of the Hall of Mirrors of Versailles, Le Brun's painting evokes the conflict. Under a flying personification of Renown holding a roll of parchment on which the legal arguments of the King are written, Louis XIV is advancing towards his troops. God Mars is showing him the path. Meanwhile the King is looking back to Lady Justice holding scales, a symbol of the morality of his cause. The child holding a torch represents god Hymen, a reminder that the war is based on dynastic rights secured through Louis XIV's marriage with a member of the Spanish royal family.

Guerre contre l'Espagne pour les Droits de la Reine

of the Western tradition to foreign types of constructions accelerated in the 19th century. Islamic architecture, but also Indian, Pre-Colombian, and Japanese, became sources of inspiration. Architectural vocabulary greatly expanded as can be gathered from the diverse grammars of ornament published along the lines of Owen Jones's seminal work.

In parallel, consensus on the nature of social authority and hierarchy crumbled under the pressure of political and class struggle. Monarchists and Republicans disagreed on the type of government suited to the industrial age. The opposition between capitalist values and working-class aspirations would lead to an even more radical conflict. The debates regarding the proper organisation of society deepened further with the development of colonial empires, with colonisation adding a racial component to the political incertitude of the period. How was one to treat foreign people and political authorities, which had been forced to recognise the domination of European countries like England or France? A simple ladder of ornamental distinction leading from sturdy to slender and from almost barren to richly adorned no longer seemed equipped to capture the complexity of the political and social field.

In such a context, communication through architectural décor became increasingly elaborate. Bosworth's or McKim, Mead & White's subtle play on the various layers of signification of the architectural orders is typical of a period in which the manipulation of ornament reached new levels of sophistication. Yet architects had to face a more daunting challenge than the adaptation of the five orders to the new programmes of the industrial era; namely, how to coordinate the use of an extended architectural vocabulary

Gian Lorenzo Bernini, St Peter's baldachin, 1634. Despite its size (its Solomonic columns are 20 metres high), the baldachin appears as a giant ornament. At the time of its creation, a lampoon castigated the Pope and his family, the Barberini, for having used the bronze of the entrance of the Pantheon for the baldachin. 'Quod non fecerunt Barbari, fecerunt Barberini': What the Barbarians did not do, the Barberini did. However, the reuse of precious material represented actually a tradition rooted in Ancient Rome's quantitative as much as qualitative approach to ornament.

Gabriel Thouin, architectural structures for gardens, from *Plans Raisonnés de toutes les Espèces de Jardins*, 1838. In the decades around 1800, garden architectural structures or *fabriques* played a major role in the diffusion of styles foreign to the Greco-Roman tradition. On Thouin's plate, one can thus see a Chinese pagoda and other exotic structures next to Greek and Roman temples.

loaded with more and more complex intentions. This is where style proved irreplaceable as a classifying and regulating mechanism. Styles enabled 19th-century theorists and practitioners to sort out ornaments according to historical, technical and aesthetic determinations. From a historical standpoint, within the society that had created them, they related natural inspiration to artificial processes, tectonic to ornament, and, above all, individual creativity to shared characteristics, both constructive and ornamental.

Definitions of style in the applied arts and architecture varied considerably from one author to another. Yet, what they had in common was the need to assign to this key notion a role of mediation between different orders of reality. In addition to connecting individual creativity to collective aesthetic choices, style linked technical determinations to intellectual and religious dispositions. Semper's famous comparison between the Egyptian Nile pail, the *situla*, and the Greek *hydria* – two ceramic vessels designed to collect water – thus began by relating their different forms to the distinction between drawing water from a river and catching the flow of a fountain. The form of the *situla* appeared as an almost literal translation of gravity constraints into pottery, whereas the *hydria* reflected a more complex set of determinations. Their respective decorations echoed these differences. According to the architect, they also expressed a more profound contrast between the submission-prone Egyptians and the 'soaring, spiritual, and lucid essence of the spring-worshipping Hellenes'.[12] For Semper, the architectural paths followed by these two peoples seemed to stem from this divergence. From pottery to architecture, styles were rooted in a complex series of interactions between the natural and the artificial, the individual and the collective, the technical and the spiritual, which defined the very essence of a civilisation.

Gottfried Semper, Egyptian *situla* and Greek *hydria*, from *Style in the Technical and Tectonic Arts; or, Practical Aesthetics*, 1860–63. The heaviest part of the *situla* is lower. It evokes a drop of water submitted to the law of gravity. The *hydria* obeys a more complex logic. It fetches water from springs, hence its generous receiving mouth. It is meant to be carried on the head, which explains its wide foot. Instead of sheer gravity, it is designed for a dynamic interplay of gravity and equilibrium.

These interactions were meant to weave a kind of net that captured the political orientation of a given society. If the comparison between two pottery vessels was enough to perceive the difference between a tendency towards submission and a spirit of freedom, the study of architecture could yield even more profound lessons. Massive Egyptian temples reflected the political views of the society that had built them, just as the more slender Greek ones expressed those held by the people behind their construction. As for Gothic cathedrals, they embodied the ideals of Western European medieval civilisation.

Now, what did the reuse of such styles come to mean in the industrial age? Historicism

Situla

Hydria

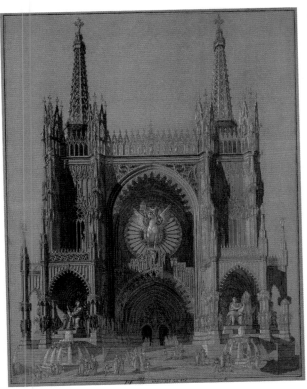

Karl Friedrich Schinkel, project for the facade of a cathedral, first half of the 19th century.
Before turning almost definitively to the Greek in his search for a style adapted to the Prussian national genius, Schinkel was tempted by the Gothic, hence his variations on the theme of the cathedral.

complicated the question of style, since it implied the manipulation of tectonic and, above all, ornamental elements beyond the scope of the context that had shaped them. Ideally, the 19th century should have been able to invent a new style corresponding to its most profound aspirations. However, what were these aspirations, exactly? The age of industry was also an age of political and social division, which seemed to doom to failure any attempt to give birth to a coherent style. In his 1828 essay, entitled *In welchem Style sollen wir bauen?* (In What Style Should We Build?), German architect Heinrich Hübsch had tried to outline the characteristics of a style for a new industrial era.[13] Despite its conceptual and formal rigour, Hübsch's attempt was not particularly successful. Similar enterprises failed for the same reason: the difficulty in reaching an artistic consensus in a period during which societies were unable to agree on the nature of their fundamental values.

What prevailed, meanwhile, was an eclectic use of historical references ranging from Ancient Egypt to the Middle Ages, and from Greece and Rome to the Renaissance and Baroque eras.

How did theorists and practitioners justify a practice that often amounted to appending ornaments borrowed from the past on present-day structures? Many 19th-century historicist monuments were actually realised using state-of-the-art technology. Even Leo von Klenze's Walhalla memorial, this re-creation of the Parthenon in Bavaria (1830–42), presented a complex iron-truss roof structure.[14] Whereas the reinterpretation of the Greco-Roman five orders could claim the legacy of the Vitruvian tradition, no comparable theoretical foundation was able to justify the apparently disparate catalogue of stylistic references that circulated throughout the 19th century, even if Viollet-le-Duc imagined convincing arguments in favour of the reuse of Gothic tectonic principles.

Viollet-le-Duc was relatively isolated in his advocacy of the 'modernity' of Gothic based on tectonic rather than ornamental considerations. The most common justification of historicism rested in an analogy between style and language, as if each style were comparable to a tongue, which possessed its own distinctive vocabulary and syntax.[15] The possibility of a 'grammar of ornament' derived precisely from this linguistic analogy. The aim was to provide the reader of this type of book with the correct notions that had governed the use of ornaments in the past.

Inseparable from the analogy between style and language was the belief that by means of a correct use of these historical ornaments, the positive values that had permeated their initial invention and deployment could be at least partly recaptured. Such conviction was in turn inseparable from the broader historicist turn of the century. Nineteenth-century philosophers, artists and even scientists firmly believed that the future was made possible by the presence of the past haunting the core of the present. History and historical materials did not only provide a measure of progress; like coal for a locomotive, they appeared as the fuel burnt by the engine that pulled the industrial society towards the future.[16]

Using historical styles enabled the convocation of specific political ideals. If the majority of architects did not share Viollet-le-Duc's enthusiastic focus on the tectonic modernity of Gothic, they generally agreed on its progressive character. Gothic architecture announced the optimism and quest for performance that characterised the industrial age. This quality enabled Victorian architect George Gilbert Scott to build the Midland Grand Hotel (1876) at St Pancras train station in Gothic Revival style, next to what was at the time the largest iron railway shed in the world. English, French and German architects also interpreted Gothic as the first truly national style. The question of whether Gothic had been invented in England, France or Germany thus appeared as a deeply contested issue.

Gothic epitomised many other perspectives, beginning with the possibility of a common faith that could bind people more efficiently than any secular constitution. Throughout the 19th century, various Christian churches used it, often with the avowed intention to reestablish the preeminence of religion over society. However, the Middle Ages could also be interpreted as the period that saw the emergence of a new secular power, with the rise of cities and the freedom they granted their burghers; hence the number of city halls and parliament houses built in a Gothic Revival idiom. Styles and

William Burges, the Arab Room, Cardiff Castle, 1881.
Whereas Oriental elements remained usually discrete on the exterior of European buildings, they could triumph without restraint in interior décors like the remarkable Arab Room of Cardiff Castle designed by William Burges for John Patrick Crichton-Stuart, 3rd Marquess of Bute. Intended as a drawing room for women, the Arab Room boasts an extraordinarily rich honeycomb ceiling reminiscent of the Alhambra.

their ornaments were both highly political and permeated with contradictory agendas. Part of their appeal lay in their ambiguity, which enabled the multiplication of implicit or double meanings like a literary text playing on the polysemy of language.

Such ambiguity was even more pronounced when the relations between the Occident and the Orient and/or between coloniser and colonised were at stake. One the one hand, Romanticism had popularised the notion of a final reconciliation and even fusion between the West and the East. On the other hand, a crude politics of dominance and the clichés of Orientalism typically took precedence over the quest for genuine cultural encounter and synthesis.[17] The hesitations that surrounded the realisation of a Crimean Memorial Church in Istanbul in the late 1850s and '60s are representative of the difficulty inherent in finding a compromise between the desire of a possible hybridisation between Western and Eastern architectural traditions and the narrow Eurocentric prejudices that colonial powers displayed most of the time beyond their historic frontiers.[18]

From Viennese Secession to Catalan Modernisme, Art Nouveau presents us with a different type of political ambiguity. It served its rich aristocrat and bourgeois patrons while exuding a diffuse anxiety that announced the end of their world. Revealingly, this anxiety reached its paroxysm in Vienna and Barcelona, the capital of a doomed empire and an industrial city marked by violent class struggle respectively, two places where 19th-century attempts at defining a new political and social order blatantly revealed their limits. Such anxiety played a role in Adolf Loos's project to get rid of ornament, as if erasing the symptom represented the first step towards what he saw as a necessary cure.

Remaining one moment with Art Nouveau, it is worth noting how décor was still at the time a natural accompaniment of planning and modernisation. There is perhaps no better illustration of such a link than the place of ornament in Otto Wagner's work for the Viennese metropolitan railway system. Around the same time, ornament was also present in the infrastructures designed by the proponents of the City Beautiful Movement in North America.

Far from being the feathers on a woman's hat mocked by Le Corbusier, styles and their ornaments were loaded with political meaning, and this

Josep Puig i Cadafalch, Café Torino, Barcelona, 1902.
A significant contribution to Catalan Modernisme, the Café Torino was conceived as a total work of art. Antoni Gaudí was involved in the design of its elaborate interior décor. Its exterior possesses a slightly disquieting character with the sculpted figure in its centre that evokes a ghost rising out of the stone.

Otto Wagner, Karlsplatz
metro station, Vienna,
1899.
With the Viennese
metropolitan railway
station, Wagner achieves an
exemplary balance between
constructive requirements
and a refined decoration
almost Secessionist in
essence.

not only through allegorical uses. Conversely, 19th- and early 20th-century politics presented a strong ornamental character. In a book devoted to the organisation of the British Empire, historian David Cannadine has shown, for example, how imperial power used an abundance of visible signs of distinctions, decorations, brilliant uniforms, horses and elephants, parades and balls, to stabilise social hierarchies at home and abroad.[19] According to him, the purpose of these various 'ornaments' was to establish a system of correspondence between the various ranks of British society and those of the foreign countries it ruled, so that a lord and a maharaja could be considered as equals. Whether Cannadine's central tenet – that the British Empire gave precedence to class rather than focusing on race and colour – is true or not does not matter here. More fundamental for our purposes is the acknowledgement that politics is as much a system of signs as it is a system of power or, rather, that it defines itself in the articulation of the two. To be believable, respected and operative at moments other than those marked by the exercise of sheer force, authority has to be adorned.

Despite early 20th-century attempts to deprive political authority of its traditional ornaments in the name of a technocratic blend of efficiency and modesty, power has remained adorned to this day. Decorations and ceremonies have endured and the codes that govern the visible expressions of power are still understandable throughout the world. From Russia to the United States and from North Korea to Brazil, parades are organised on a regular basis, while presidents and generals have to wear tuxedos and uniforms as part of their functions. By contrast, architecture has lost its ornaments, and Modernism has not been able to achieve the same degree of institutional clarity as that achieved by neo-Greek colonnades and Gothic Revival churches. One of the major strengths of 19th-century architecture lay in its legibility, which was to a large extent based on a linguistic interpretation of style and ornament.

In this respect, the shortcomings of modern architecture are nowhere more evident than in a place like Washington DC where the use of the Classical orders went on well into the 20th century. While referring itself to former periods such as the Renaissance and Baroque, Postmodernism actually tried to resurrect something like the 19th-century linguistic use of architectural elements, but at the same time it confused ornament with a frozen symbol borrowed from the past or from vernacular culture instead of interpreting it as a dynamic operator. Despite its critique of the Modernist infatuation with tectonic articulation and its plea for the reinvention of décor, Postmodernism was not able to revive the logic of supplementarity which had characterised ornament until the dawn of Modernism.

The King of the Asante and the Governor of the Gold Coast, 1935. According to historian David Cannadine, the British Empire was based on a system of visual and social equivalences between the metropolitan and foreign distinctions and classes. Here, the ruler of the Ashanti people and the Governor of the Gold Coast, present-day Ghana, are presented as peers.

The Power of Architectural Décor

Communication is not the only dimension at stake when one tries to grasp what constitutes the political relevance of ornament. The latter possesses also the capacity to make the world a hospitable place through the composition of immersive décors. The notion of décor deserves at this stage a more thorough examination. It is interesting to note that the English term derives from the French and was linked to the theatre. Its French equivalent is still used to designate stage sets.

The interaction between ornaments produces décor. This interaction can be related to the existence of a tectonic frame on which ornaments are applied like a commentary of its main articulations, or conversely by the negation of such a frame in favour of a purely ornamental regime. What matters is that décor seems to hold the ornaments together, to integrate them into a coherent system. However, the integration is always partial and fragile, as the illusion produced by a stage set, for décor also reveals the fundamental duality of ornamentation. On the one hand, ornamentation points towards the possibility of a rational order based on notions such as proportion, rhythm, tectonic. On the other hand, it constantly challenges the very possibility of such an order by its capacity to overstep any predetermined point of equilibrium and boundary. Décor is always the result of a compromise between not enough and too much. It appears sometimes as a background against which ornament stands out, more often as the system of interrelations between the various ornaments that constitute it; but it can

Félix Duban, architectural fantasy in the Pompeian style, 1856.
In this very graphic composition, French architect Félix Duban (1797–1870) captures two essential features of décor. On the one hand, they are coordinated so as to constitute a coherent whole; on the other hand, some of these ornaments challenged the order thus achieved. Fruits piled in the cup in the centre are about to spill. More generally, overabundance represents a constant threat, and one may lose oneself in the details of the composition and forget about its overall organisation. As a practising architect, Duban designed a number of stately decorative schemes, beginning with those of the New Louvre of Napoleon III.

also result from an ornamental profusion, which challenges any preconceived notion of coordination.

Man inhabits décors. In a remarkable meditation on architecture, French philosopher Pierre Caye argues that the project of the Renaissance founding fathers of the discipline, such as Leon Battista Alberti or Daniele Barbaro, was to shelter man from the violence of the infinite to preserve his sanity. Conceived as a décor, the role of architecture was to install humanity into an intermediary world between nature and the gods, between pure immanence and radical transcendence, while offering a glimpse of the two.[20] If we retain this perspective, ornament appears indispensable as a means of generating the arena in which human actions and history can unfold. Ornament not only communicates about politics; it represents one of its preconditions by delimiting the space it needs for its deployment.

Vincenzo Scamozzi, detail of trompe-l'oeil of the scenery of the Teatro Olimpico in Vicenza, Italy, 1585.
In what is probably the oldest surviving stage set in Europe, Scamozzi evokes a measured and adorned world, a perfect décor for meaningful human actions.

It is useful to return to Oleg Grabar and his proposition that we should consider architecture as ornament, or rather as décor in the sense evoked here. For Grabar, one must acknowledge 'the more profound truth of architecture in general, that it is always at the service of man and has no greater purpose than to adorn his manifold activities, something as simple and prosaic as eating or listening to a lecture and something as glorious as worshiping God or contemplating a work of art'.[21] Politics, which combine the simple and prosaic with the glorious, ranks among these activities.

Another way to understand the role of décor is to think of how some very frequent business travellers – 'neo-nomads', to use architect Yasmine Abbas's characterisation – make themselves at home all over the world by customising their hotel rooms with a few selected objects, a small clock, one or two pictures in a frame.[22] Such familiar objects are comparable to ornaments, which can transform an anonymous space into a personal retreat. Without ornament and its capacity to generate décor, the world would be impersonal and likely uninhabitable.

Andrea Pozzo, trompe-l'oeil ceiling of Sant'Ignazio in Rome, after 1685.
In this grandiose fresco, Andrea Pozzo, a Jesuit brother, celebrates the accomplishments of Saint Ignatius and the Society of Jesus founded by him. This immersive Baroque décor depicts the reception of the Saint in Paradise.

From Roman frescoes to Baroque painted ceilings, the development of architecture has been marked by a series of spectacular décors, some of them imparted with an immersive character, which we tend to associate today with new electronic worlds, as if immersivity were not one of the oldest characteristics of built environments. Charles Garnier's majestic Grand Staircase of the Paris Opera (1875), the setting of so many French official ceremonies, offers perhaps one of the best illustrations of the political relevance of such immersive décors.

Ornament is often political and politics needs decoration. This complementarity could very well be rooted in an enduring ornamental impulse that Modernism was never able to eradicate. The fundamental paradox of ornamentation deepens. Ornament is not only added and at the same time essential; as soon as we begin to think that we have circumscribed it, we realise that we are actually surrounded by it. Actually, we are not only surrounded by décor; we are also permeated by ornament. We try to adorn our minds, just as we tend to decorate our lives and actions.

Édouard Detaille, reception of the Lord Mayor of London by Charles Garnier on 5 January 1875.
The reception takes place on the monumental staircase of the new Opera of Paris recently completed by Charles Garnier. On such formal occasions, the political relevance of the décor designed by the architect becomes especially evident.

References

1 Cf Yael Reisner, Fleur Watson, *Architecture and Beauty* (Chichester, West Sussex: John Wiley & Sons, 2010).

2 Pierre Bullet, *L'Architecture Pratique* (Paris: E Michallet, 1691), pp 141–59.

3 Patricia Falguières, 'L'Ornement du Droit', presentation given on 7 November 2011 at the conference *Questionner l'Ornement*, organised by the Arts Décoratifs and the Institut National d'Histoire de l'Art in Paris on 7–8 November 2011.

4 Jacques-François Blondel, *Cours d'Architecture* (Paris: Desaint, 1771-7), t1, pp 216–19.

5 Antoine Picon, *Claude Perrault 1613-1688 ou la Curiosité d'un Classique* (Paris: Picard,1988), p 189 in particular. On the attempt to create a French order, see also Jean-Marie Pérouse de Montclos, 'Le Sixième Ordre d'Architecture, ou la Pratique des Ordres Suivant les Nations', *Journal of the Society of Architectural Historians*, vol 36, no 4, 1977, pp 223–40.

6 Cf Barry Bergdoll, *Karl Friedrich Schinkel: An Architecture for Prussia* (New York: Rizzoli, 1994).

7 Mark Jarzombek, *Designing MIT: The Architecture of William Welles Bosworth* (Boston, MA: Northeastern University Press, October 2004).

8 Steven Parissien, *McKim, Mead and White: Pennsylvania Station New York 1905–10* (London: Phaidon, 1996).

9 See for instance Werner Oechslin, Anja Buschow, *Architecture de Fête: L'Architecte comme Metteur en Scène* (Brussels: Mardaga, 1984).

10 On the décor of Versailles, see Gérard Sabatier, *Versailles ou la Figure du Roi* (Paris: Albin Michel, 1999).

11 French historian Michèle Fogel has captured the role of communication in Ancien Régime France remarkably in her book *Les Cérémonies de l'Information dans la France du XVIe au XVIIIe Siècle* (Paris: Fayard, 1989). Throughout the early modern period, architectural ornament can be interpreted as a component of the 'ceremonies of information' evoked by Michèle Fogel.

12 Gottfried Semper, *Style in the Technical and Tectonic Arts; or, Practical Aesthetics* (Frankfurt, Munich, 1860–63, English trs, Los Angeles: Getty Research Institute, 2004), p 469. For a more detailed analysis of Semper's parallel, see Mari Hvattum, *Gottfried Semper and the Problem of Historicism* (Cambridge: Cambridge University Press, 2004), pp 110–11 in particular.

13 Heinrich Hübsch, *In What Style Should We Build? The German Debate on Architectural Style* (Los Angeles: Getty Center for the History of Art and the Humanities, 1992).

14 Winfried Nerdinger (ed), *Leo von Klenze: Architekt zwischen Kunst und Hof, 1784–1864* (Munich: Prestel, 2000).

15 See on this question Anthony Alofsin, *When Buildings Speak: Architecture as Language in the Habsburg Empire and its Aftermath, 1867–1933* (Chicago, London: The

University of Chicago Press, 2006).

16 See on this theme Philippe Muray, *Le XIXe Siècle à travers les Ages* (Paris: Gallimard, 1999).

17 See for instance Nabila Oulebsir, Mercedes Volait (eds), *L'Orientalisme Architectural: Entre Imaginaires et Savoirs* (Paris: CNRS, Picard, 2009).

18 Mark Crinson, *Empire Building: Orientalism and Victorian Architecture* (New York: Routledge, 1996), pp 138–66.

19 David Cannadine, *Ornamentalism: How the British saw their Empire* (Oxford, New York: Oxford University Press, 2001).

20 Pierre Caye, *Empire et Décor: L'Architecture et la Question de la Technique à l'Age Humaniste et Classique* (Paris: Vrin, 1999).

21 Oleg Grabar, *The Mediation of Ornament* (Princeton: Princeton University Press, 1992), p 193.

22 Yasmine Abbas, *Le Néo-Nomadisme: Mobilités, Partage, Transformations Identitaires et Urbaines* (Limoges: FYP, 2011).

Reinventing the Meaning of Ornament

4

In direct relation to the development of digital culture, ornament has returned. Projects as different as UN Studio's Galleria Department Store facade in Seoul (2004) and Manuelle Gautrand's extension of the Lille Museum of Modern, Contemporary and Outsider Art (2009) present a strong manifestation of this phenomenon. After discussing at length the gap between yesterday and today, between the decorative tradition that prevailed until the dawn of Modernism and the contemporary ornamental trend, the time has come to examine how they are nonetheless related through issues pertaining to subjectivity and politics.

A New Architectural Subject

The subjective dimension does not seem initially obvious, given the abstract character of many present-day ornaments. We are not immediately reminded of a visage when looking at textures, patterns or topological structures. If its relation to subjectivity doesn't stand out, today's ornament appears instead strongly indebted to an inquiry regarding materiality and the human senses. Under the influence of a series of factors ranging from the spectacular development of material sciences to the rise of the computer and the possibilities it offers to visualise and operate at various levels, from macroscopic to nanoscopic scales, our understanding of materiality is evolving rapidly. Contemporary architectural ornament is inseparable from this general

UN Studio, Galleria Department Store facade, Seoul, South Korea, 2004. The new facade is made of 4,330 glass discs mounted on the existing concrete skin of the building. These discs incorporate a special dichroic foil which generates a mother-of-pearl effect during the day. At night, LED lights create a wide variety of visual effects. The facade can respond in particular to the dynamics of atmospheric conditions.

movement. Its appeal owes something to the desire to experiment in a field, which looks more and more like a new frontier for design and manufacture.[1] It is no coincidence that so many material investigations in architecture present an ornamental character, from Gramazio and Kohler's robotic assemblages to Neri Oxman's explorations of the new permeability between the natural and the computable.

Actually, the notion of materiality provides us with a first clue regarding the renewed importance of subjectivity. For materiality, unlike matter, can

Manuelle Gautrand, extension of the Lille Museum of Modern, Contemporary and Outsider Art, Villeneuve-d'Ascq, 2009. Manuelle Gautrand's project is an addition to an existing building by Roland Simounet dedicated to a collection of Art Brut works. The thin envelope is made of Ductal, a high-performance fibre-reinforced concrete with a smooth finish. The ornamental screens are meant to modulate daylight and the visual relation of the interior to the surrounding park. The precious effect they produce is inseparable from the technical properties of the concrete.

never be considered as entirely objective. Materiality corresponds to a certain category of experience. The point becomes more evident when one considers its opposite, immateriality. Nothing is in itself immaterial. We call something immaterial when we cannot relate to it in certain ways – by seeing it with our own eyes or with the help of instruments that we trust, for instance. Conversely, materiality corresponds to a range of experiences that give us the impression of being in genuine contact with the physical world. Some of these experiences are based on immediate sensory evidence; others involve instruments and machines, binoculars, microscopes or computers. Whatever the case, materiality possesses a relational character. It implies an encounter between a subject and the material world.

From this perspective, materiality appears as a mix of permanent ahistorical features and cultural factors. At any given time, materiality articulates physical constraints, such as the laws of mechanics or the physiology of perception as well as social constructs such as the value we attach to certain types of observations. For the 17th-century adversaries of Galileo, the images of the moon he had obtained by looking through a telescope were immaterial.[2]

They would become material with the triumph of the scientific revolution. Similarly, the new generations of 'digital natives' no longer perceive computer imagery as immaterial.[3]

Designed and fabricated with the help of the computer, contemporary ornamentation is inseparable from an inquiry into our rapidly changing definition of materiality. In connection with this inquiry, it presents a number of revealing features. First, it appeals strongly to the senses, to a mix of sight and touch in particular, which gives the impression of engaging the whole sensorium. The tactile dimension is evident in the case of Herzog & de Meuron's De Young Museum with its dots that evoke a text written in Braille. With their intriguing textures, many other projects invite the viewer to stroke their facades with his/her fingertips. Tactility reached its climax with the now dismantled Heatherwick Studio's UK Pavilion at Shanghai 2010 Expo and its 60,000 acrylic rods that evoked a giant fur ball.

This haptic character often goes together with a visual complexity that borders the hypnotic. The swirls and tendrils of Foreign Office Architects'

Gramazio & Kohler, Architecture and Digital Fabrication, ETH Zurich, The Sequential Wall, 2008. In their experiments on architecture and digital fabrication, Fabio Gramazio and Matthias Kohler at ETH Zurich often create structures with a marked ornamental character.

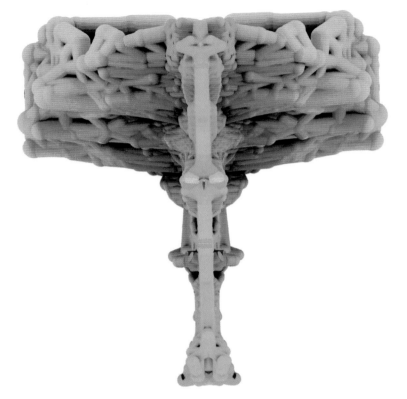

Neri Oxman, Fate Maps, 2008.
The sculpture derives from an investigation into the conditions that govern the formation of materials and tissues at the intersection of design, computation and biology. Through this type of research, Neri Oxman's objective is to facilitate the emergence of a 'new materialism' in architecture and design.

John Lewis department store present a hypnotic quality. Studio 505's Pixel building in Melbourne (2010) likewise captivates the eye with its coloured panels that remind the spectator of a cybernetic sculpture of the 1960s, a Nicolas Schöffer creation, for instance. More generally, contemporary ornament often seems to take after the artistic experiments of the 1950s and '60s, from cybernetic to Op art. Its textures, patterns, curves and folds look animated. Like many of the experiments in the 1950s and '60s, it tends to address perception as a whole, at the level of the sensorium rather than through isolated channels.

From the accent put on the tactile to the almost hypnotic effects of superficial visual complexity, what seems fundamentally at stake is a destabilisation of the traditional distinction between subject and object, as if the viewer and the architectural work were part of a single continuum. Such a continuum is anti-perspectival in that it abolishes the notion of a privileged point of view from which one should contemplate the building. Perspective implied a distance between the observer and the scene or the object observed, a distance that is no longer relevant if seeing becomes akin to touching. The traditional distinction between ornament and décor also fades. Like décor, contemporary digital ornament functions in an immersive way. The recurring analogy drawn by critics between Baroque and digital design might have to do not only with their eventful geometries, but also with the immersive tendencies, which they both display.[4]

To convey this new regime of relation between architecture and its viewers, today's designers readily refer themselves to the Deleuzian notion of affect. In their book on ornament, Farshid Moussavi and Michael Kubo consider, for instance, that the main purpose of contemporary architectural décor lies in the production of affect.[5] According to Gilles Deleuze, affects are not attached to a subject's mind in the way personal feelings are. Of a much more physical nature, they denote a change in intensity that concerns both the body and its surrounding space and time. From this perspective, affects represent a more primitive form of experience than emotions. Contrary to emotions that presuppose a localised psychological interiority, affects appear linked to a kind of generic superficial condition. They are both superficial and immersive, two features that correspond especially well to the characteristics of present-day ornament.

The Deleuzian reference reveals itself inseparable from an approach to the relation between the subject and the world based on their continuity. The subject, if one may still use this term, can no longer be envisaged as a separate substance; rather, it appears as a kind of inflexion or as a zone of

Heatherwick Studio's UK Pavilion at Shanghai 2010 Expo.
Known by the public as the Seed Cathedral, the UK Pavilion at Shanghai 2010 Expo housed some 60,000 plant seeds at the end of acrylic rods. The stunning effect produced by the hairy object blurred the boundary between the visual and the tactile.

Snøhetta, Norwegian
Wild Reindeer Centre
Pavilion, Tverrfjellhytta,
2011.
Located on the outskirts
of the Dovrefjell National
Park, at an altitude of 1,200
metres above the sea, the
project is based on the
contrast between a rigid
outer shell and an organic
inner core. Using natural
materials such as wood,
the core may be interpreted
alternatively as architecture,
furniture or ornament. Here
also, tactility represents
a major dimension of the
design.

peculiar intensity in a field. This conception leads to placing the accent on
entities like forces, fields, flows and gradients, and on actions like twisting,
bending and folding. The analogy between such a vocabulary and the type
of formal manipulation fostered by computer software ranks among the
reasons that Gilles Deleuze's philosophy is so attractive to digital designers,
even if the attention paid initially by someone like Greg Lynn to the figure
of the fold and to Deleuze's eponymous book predated widespread use of
the computer in architecture.[6]

In addition to continuity, multiplicity and complexity represent other key
aspects of the Deleuzian heritage. Contrary to the Cartesian subject, the
Deleuzian individual looks inherently manifold and complex, rhizomatic or
network-like. Again, these figures prove admirably adapted to the play upon
textures, patterns and topology that characterises the envelope of so many
digital projects. Rather than evoking a traditional visage, contemporary
ornament seems to offer a glimpse into a labyrinthine set of modules,
connections and processes. No longer comparable to a mask, the skin
becomes analogous to a permeable interface, an osmotic membrane.

Foreign Office Architects, John Lewis department store, Leicester, 2007. The swirls of the facade present an almost hypnotic character, not so far removed from the effects aimed at by cybernetic or Op art in the 1950s and '60s.

Studio 505, Pixel building, Melbourne, Australia, 2010. The building is Australia's first carbon-neutral office building. Its coloured panels provide view, light and glare control. Made of recycled material, they are supported by spandrels which provide shading and grey-water treatment. The project is emblematic of the close association between ornament and environment-friendly envelope performativity that characterises many contemporary design approaches.

Late cyberneticists like Gregory Bateson had also raised the issue of an inherently multiple subject in continuity with his environment.[7] Echoes of this conception are still detectable in Bruno Latour's or Peter Sloterdijk's writings, through their insistence on the multiple mediations that relate individuals to the world and seem almost literally to distribute their identities along various canals.[8] Their influence in the design world testifies to the actuality of the question. Above all, contemporary science and technology lend credibility to such a vision day after day. The neurosciences have broken, for instance, with the classical interpretation of the brain as a unified information processor and see its activity, probably including self-consciousness, as the result of a series of complex interactions within layered networks. From this perspective, we are akin to environments, 'ecologies'.

With the rise of digital culture, the idea that we are inherently manifold and difficult to separate from our environment has taken a new turn. Indeed, our identity seems to flow outside our body into the myriads of cyber arteries and veins that connect us to others. With the multiplication of such canals, we need no longer stick to Japanese architect Toyo Ito's proposition that we, of the age of Internet, possess two bodies: one made of flesh, the other of electrons.[9] We are no longer cyborgs obtained through a crude collage of flesh and technology, but existences finely distributed within various meshes, which articulate almost seamlessly the biological and the electronic.

Does this distributed mode of existence still allow us to speak of a human subject? Fuelled by postmodern philosophy, by the most recent progress of

Thomas Deerinck, NCMIR/ Science Photo Library, synapse nerve junctions. A coloured scanning electron micrograph of nerve cells showing the synapses between them. At the synapse, an electrical signal is transmitted from one cell to the next in only one direction. When an electrical signal reaches a synapse it triggers the release of neurotransmitter chemicals contained in the yellow vesicles visible on the image. We are network-like, from the microstructure of our brains to the macro level of our involvement in an ever-increasing number of technological and social systems.

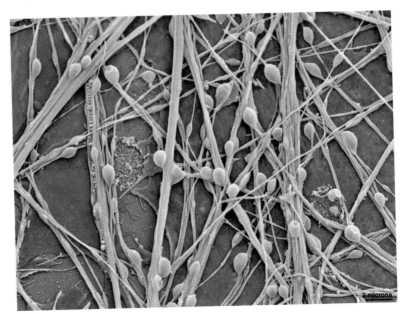

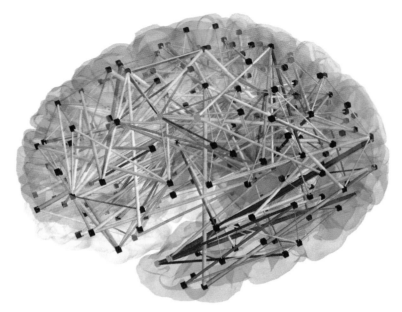

Stephan Gerhard, Patric Hagmann, Jean-Philippe Thiran, Connectome Mapping Toolkit, Ecole Polytechnique Fédérale de Lausanne and Université de Lausanne, Switzerland, 2010.
A connectome is a comprehensive map of the neural connections in the brain. At the EPFL, a team has been working on the production of an open-source framework to manage, analyse and visualise connectomes. At this level also, we appear inherently multiple, network-like.

31.25 Mpc/h

Volker Springel, Simon DM White, Adrian Jenkins, Carlos S Frenk, Naoki Yoshida, Liang Gao, Julio Navarro, Robert Thacker, Darren Croton, John Helly, John A Peacock, Shaun Cole, Peter Thomas, Hugh Couchman, August Evrard, Joerg Colberg, Frazer Pearce, simulation of the joint evolution of quasars, galaxies and their large-scale distribution, 2005.
Visually, the universe described by contemporary astrophysics strangely resembles the world of neurosciences.

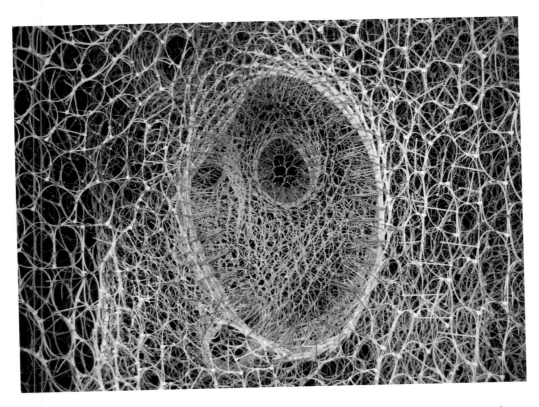

Sabin + Jones
LabStudio, 'Branching
Morphogenesis', 2008.
Involving a mix of designers
and scientists, the project
explores fundamental
processes in living systems
with the objective of finding
potential applications in
architecture. Interestingly,
this type of interdisciplinary
research with strong design
and computing dimensions
presents an ornamental
character.

a more and more intrusive technology as well as by artistic endeavours such
as Stelarc's or Orlan's attempts to modify and extend the human body, the
literature on the posthuman represents a thriving genre.[10] In architecture,
Andrew Benjamin suggested a few years ago that interrogating, if not
destroying, the subject was among the key features of recent design evolution.[11]

Online life is again revealing. On the one hand, as sociologist Sherry Turkle
has observed, multitasking, the shorter and shorter attention span generated
by intensive browsing and the accumulation of identities, tend to blur the
traditional definitions of identity and personality.[12] We are indeed manifold
with the ever-increasing trail of usernames, passwords and avatars that
follow us on the Internet. On the other hand, however, we tend also to
reconstruct more stable representations of ourselves through homepages and
blogs. We definitely try to appear as fully-fledged subjects on Facebook and
LinkedIn. Distribution and dispersion are perhaps not sufficient to characterise

contemporary subjectivity. It may prove preferable to approach it in terms of a constant pulsation, a movement of expansion followed by a tendency to contract in order to resemble once more a traditional subject.

In this constant beat, the role played by ornamental practices is equally telling. Taken in a broad sense, ornament exerts a dissolving power on individuality and subjectivity. From reality shows to advertisements, we bathe in an ocean of ornaments that produce anonymity. The collective rituals to which they correspond are not without analogy to popular entertainment, which inspired Siegfried Kracauer's famous analysis of the 'mass ornament'.[13] We might be facing a new and hysterical version of the 'mass ornament'. Whether truly postmodern or not – French sociologist François Ascher found it, for his part, rather hypermodern – our society reveals itself intensely ornamental.[14]

Yet, ornament is also mobilised to reconstruct a highly personal approach to the world. No matter that some ornamental practices, like piercing and tattoos, actually present a mass character, the aim is usually to assert one's identity and unique vision. The proliferation of tattoos proves especially

LAB Architecture Studio, Federation Square atrium, Melbourne, Australia, 2003.
With its complex folded geometries following a triangular pinwheel tiling pattern, the glass walls of the Melbourne Federation Square atrium seem to echo the labyrinthine character of contemporary subjectivity.

Hajime Masubuchi and
Thom Faulders, Airspace,
Tokyo, Japan, 2007.
A porous, multilayered
meshwork facade designed
with the ambition to rival
nature by providing an
interface with properties
similar to a layer of dense
vegetation. The layering
constitutes an answer to the
building's inner organisation.
It creates a zone where the
artificial blends with nature.

remarkable from this perspective. Our streets are full of young queens and
warriors adorned in a manner that would have horrified Adolf Loos, although
he would have been slightly reassured by its dependence upon social class.
Despite what some scholars have called a 'tattoo renaissance', children of the
middle and upper classes still seem less prone to get tattooed than offspring
of the working classes.[15]

Where does architectural ornament fit into this broad picture? As we have
seen, it relates clearly to the new form of subjectivity that is emerging before
our very eyes. It expresses some of its most fundamental features, such as its
seamless integration within its environment, its multiplicity and complexity.
The new superficial condition of architecture that it epitomises also echoes
a propensity to live and perform at the surface of things and beings, which
has been noted by philosophers and cultural thinkers such as Jean-François
Lyotard or Fredric Jameson. Jameson, in particular, has observed how in many

postmodern productions, 'depth is replaced by surface or by multiple surfaces'.[16] Whether post- or hypermodern, the contemporary subject similarly displays a marked tendency to recognise textures and patterns rather than forms and structures.

However, does the role of architectural ornament extend beyond this expressive function? Does it directly participate in the deconstruction/reconstruction of subjectivity, in response to this fundamental beat or pulse? So far, the effectiveness of contemporary architectural décor seems to lie primarily in pleasurable affects. To be more precise, the viewer finds himself exposed to alternatives of almost subliminal enjoyment and conscious realisation that ornament provokes changes in himself and his relation to the architectural object. Such alternatives are not without analogy to the way in music one can almost simultaneously experience music in a pre-subjective state that dissolves the distinction between the self and the world, and enrol it to heighten one's level of self-consciousness. There is something musical in contemporary architectural ornament.

Alan Antiporda, Illusive Photography, Chrissy, 2010.
Today, tattoo represents more than ever a means of individual affirmation. One may wonder to what extent contemporary architectural ornament does not correspond to a kind of extended tattooed condition.

There are still incomplete and missing dimensions today. In the first chapter of this book, we proposed to read ornament under a triple light: as connected to pleasure, but also to social distinction and knowledge. If ornamental pleasure has returned, the relation between contemporary décor and social ranking and prestige remains tainted with ambiguity. As for the link with knowledge, it appears almost completely absent.

Present-day architectural ornaments connect to questions of social ranking through the type of programme they usually adorn: prestigious museums, stadiums and theatres, high-end offices and condominiums. Yet, no clear gradation exists leading from monuments and luxurious programmes to modest buildings. When the budget allows for it, an architect will use the same type of texturing and patterning for social housing as for a museum. The neutrality of architectural décor with respect to social hierarchy, which used to represent a fundamental role of ornamentation, is troubling. One may interpret it as a manifestation of social generosity; it is more probably

Martin Bechthold, marble surfacing studies done with a robotic arm at the Harvard Graduate School of Design, 2008.
The study focuses on the use of a robotically controlled abrasive-waterjet cutter to shape marble through CNC machining. This exploration reveals new material effects such as translucency. Computer fabrication gives the impression of reconnecting with a long-gone artisanal dimension. However, the question of the relation between design and labour remains unanswered.

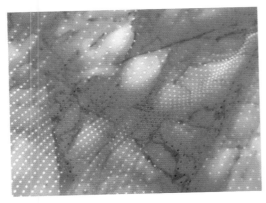

dictated by a feeling of helplessness, when faced with having to distinguish and differentiate in a society paradoxically more and more inegalitarian.

The very generic nature of the subject targeted by today's architectural décor proves even more problematic. Contrary to tattoos, which are associated with relatively specific profiles, architectural ornaments do not have clear addressees. Neither rich nor poor, neither educated nor uneducated – it does not really matter – the contemporary subject of architecture seems deprived of any specific social character. The only element of certitude lies in his/her intimate connection with the designer. It is as if the figure of the architect had replaced all the other players, artist, artisan and client. The eclipse of the artisan is especially noticeable. Strangely enough, given the attention paid by the author of *The Seven Lamps of Architecture* to the worker's prerogatives, the artisan has disappeared from the stage in the name of a 'digital Ruskinism', which posits the designer as the new craftsman of the age of computer-aided fabrication. Along with Semper, Ruskin represents a common reference for digital designers because of the accent he puts on materiality and craft, but his discourse on the dignity of labour has fallen into oblivion.[17] In the current discourses on 'non-standard' fabrication, nothing exists besides the hand of the designer moving a mouse in front of a screen and the machines milling materials according to his specifications.[18]

The lack of relation between contemporary architectural ornament and knowledge is far more conspicuous than the paucity of its social relevance. The predominance of affect appears directly responsible for this shortcoming. There is, of course, nothing intrinsically problematic in calling upon affect, if other levels of reference complement its contribution to architectural expression. However, when affect reigns supreme, architecture may risk losing its capacity to be on the verge of speaking. Again, buildings never speak, but part of their appeal lies in the impression that they could if the proper conditions were met.

Political Uncertainties

The ornamental triad – pleasure, social distinction and knowledge – was instrumental in the articulation of the subjective with the political. The ambiguities that plague them today may have to do with the political uncertainty that digital architecture has to confront despite its ambition to be as politically relevant as its forerunners. Part of the uncertainty comes from the questions left unanswered by affect. What type of political order does it presuppose? Does it even imply a social bond between the people it concerns? Of course, one may consider that such a bond exists, and that it lies in shared pleasure, as if architecture were only enjoyable as a collective and somewhat passive spectacle. From this perspective, one could invoke again the analogy between ornament and music. Is this, however, enough? Should one remain confined to a politics of affect?

Modern architecture complemented its use of affect by a discourse on function and by ideals of technological and social progress combined with a genuine concern for the natural dimension of life. The performalist attitude adopted by so many contemporary digital designers, which might eventually replace functionalism, has not yet reached a sufficient degree of maturity.[19] It is not enough to envisage architecture in terms of how buildings behave and what they produce. The question remains of how performalism translates concretely in the design process. As for the values that could substitute themselves for the former faith in progress, apart perhaps from the rising concern for sustainability, the least one can say is that they remain unclear.

Of course, the problem does not lie at the level of political parties and programmes. One should not reduce the relation between architecture and politics to the ideological role that it has played at certain moments in history, albeit not always successfully. One may even wonder if reinventing general values comparable to the Modernist faith in progress represents the ultimate issue in all this. Architecture is often at its best when the message that it conveys remains ambiguous. Oleg Grabar probably offers a better avenue to explore with his suggestion that architecture's vocation is to constitute 'an invitation to behave in certain ways' by the sheer virtue of the setting that it creates. To behave in certain ways and in interaction with others: it is difficult not to be reminded of Schinkel's famous characterisation of the architect as 'the ennobler of all human relationships'.[20] Another way to express the same idea could be to define architecture as an incentive to act in a meaningful way.

How can architecture trigger meaning? There have been multiple answers to this question, from 19th-century historicist doctrines to 20th-century phenomenological approaches. Towards the end of the Modernist period, the issue had acquired certain urgency. Published in 1970, Charles Jencks and George Baird's collection of essays, *Meaning in Architecture*, offered a comprehensive panorama of the attempts made to define a notion that proved as elusive as it was enticing.[21] Since that time, meaning has been discarded because of the excesses to which it had led, such as crude historicism or cheap symbolism. In this trial, Postmodernism was an obvious culprit and many designers swore never to make the same mistakes again. Digital architecture, in particular, rejected meaning as leading to unnecessary additions, which confused the train of affects that architecture was supposed to convey. The time has perhaps come to reexamine the question more closely. Without reinventing Postmodernism, it may be useful to rediscover some of the issues that it raised, beginning with the quest for a renewed legibility of architecture.

Meaning and Symbols

Meaning is still officially taboo, but what is one to make of so many iconic projects that seem to indulge in an almost naive form of symbolism? Retrospectively, one may consider that Jean Nouvel's Institut du Monde Arabe (1987) opened a new era of symbolic manipulation with the sunscreens of its main facade, which played on a mix of references including traditional Arabic mashrabiyas. Almost Orientalist, the use of Islamic-inspired decorative patterns has continued to this day with highlights such as OMA's project for the New

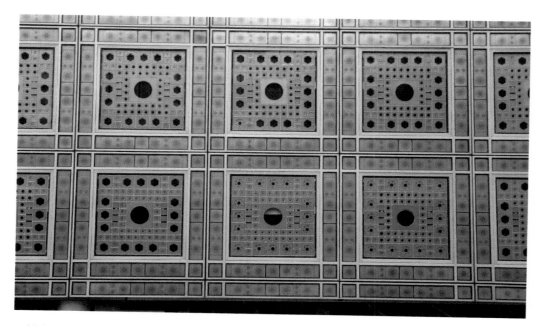

Jeddah International Airport (2005). Other symbolic references to nature, art or technology have appeared in various adorned buildings. In some 'green' buildings, trees and other vegetal elements seem also to play a symbolic role, and this all the more since the designer has placed them in both highly visible and improbable positions, like trophies meant to celebrate the victory of sustainability upon industrial philistinism. Robert Levit clearly has a point when he evokes 'the return of the symbolic repressed' in the use of ornament.[22]

Irresistible as it may appear, the return of the symbolic repressed remains largely unacknowledged and untheorised. In these circumstances, there is a serious risk of falling back into easy symbolism. The best way to avoid this lies in a reexamination of the question of meaning in architecture. Such reexamination may appear as a manifestation of a more general need for the architectural discipline to break with presentism and reconnect with a sense of history that has been eclipsed by the rapid development of the digital. Whatever judgement one may be tempted to pass upon Patrik Schumacher's ambition to resurrect the notion of style in order to theorise 'Parametricism', one must recognise the role played by history in his endeavour.[23] Until recently, such an intensive mobilisation of historical references by a practitioner would have been almost impossible.

Jean Nouvel, Institut du Monde Arabe, Paris, 1987. The facade designed by Jean Nouvel possesses a remarkable evocative power. Even if the range of references extends from camera diaphragms to computer chips, one retains an overall impression of preciosity that is reminiscent of a mythical and adorned Orient. It is as if this mythical Orient were joining forces with high-tech, a suggestion definitely in line with the vocation of the building to showcase the vitality of Arab culture.

Despite its seduction, the concept of style might not reveal itself the most appropriate to present-day challenges. We are neither confronted with problems of coordination between tectonic and ornament – ornament seems to have won – nor with an ever-expanding catalogue of decorative elements borrowed from the past. Meaning is no longer threatening because of a potentially cancerous proliferation. The difficulty lies in determining what type of message architecture should convey and how.

Useful precedents are not provided by 19th-century allegories. It seems difficult, to say the least, to imagine that architecture will again be adorned with symbolic figures like Carpeaux's *Imperial France Bringing Light to the World and Protecting Agriculture and Science*. Robert Venturi's billboards or today's giant digital screens may represent a better type of solution, but they come generally after and with little or no connection to the architectural form.

OMA, project for the New Jeddah International Airport, 2005.
The intricate embroideries of the skin make explicit reference to the decorative patterns of traditional Arabic architecture. They seem to contradict the claim that contemporary ornament is no longer symbolic.

At this point, it may be profitable to revisit once again the five orders of the Vitruvian tradition. The point is definitely not to advocate their return, in the manner of Postmodernism. Charles Moore and Perez Architects' Piazza d'Italia colonnades in downtown New Orleans (1978) no longer appeal to us, and this is probably for the best. Although the fundamental codes of Greco-Roman-inspired architecture are still highly recognisable by lay people, they do not offer a viable solution to computer-aided design conundrums.

What remains truly fascinating, in the case of the orders, is how they were both abstract, and invested with definite symbolic content. This double character was especially pronounced in the case of the Tuscan, Doric and Ionic, which comprised no elements taken directly from nature, at least in their generic form, contrary to the Corinthian and Composite with their acanthus leaves. Instead of being based on imitation, the analogy between the orders and the human body stemmed from a mix of intuition and cultural convention. Of course, the solidity of the Doric shaft could evoke masculinity, whereas the slender Ionic seemed closer to feminine proportions; but the connection was anything but deterministic. It was as much a cultural legacy and convention as a perception. Nothing in the Doric and Ionic resembled human bodies. Actually, the only anthropomorphic type of column, the so-called Caryatid order, played a marginal role in the Vitruvian tradition.

What the example of the orders tends to suggest is that architectural symbolism does not necessarily entail a return to representation, or at least to indisputable analogy. Symbolism may also lie in the emergence of a possible resemblance, at the articulation of perception and culture, rather than in a static set of imitative features. Just as architecture should always look as

MVRDV, 3D Garden, Boom Hengelo, Hengelo, Netherlands, 1999. What is the exact status of nature in this project, which transposes to housing the principle of the suspended forest tested by the architects for the Dutch Pavilion of Hanover Expo 2000? Trees might be nothing more than giant ornaments imparted with a clear symbolic function.

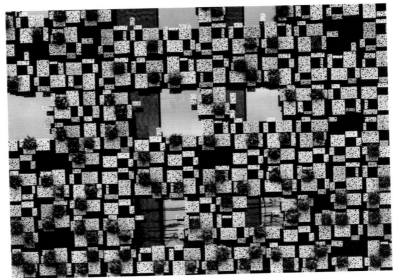

if it were about to speak, all the while remaining utterly silent, the most powerful architectural symbols are perhaps those engaged in the process of representing something. What they truly embody is a movement towards representation, a dynamic captured in the material of the building, something like a figure on the verge of appearing.

Another stimulating aspect of the five orders is how they related to a set of highly formalised mathematical operations. Their dependence on proportion and eurythmic considerations constituted rules, namely practical principles of operativity rooted in the firm belief that the world we inhabit can acquire a sense for humanity. The orders suggested the possibility of a rewarding framework for man and society. This type of suggestion represents perhaps the best way for architecture to demonstrate its political relevance. What we need today are rules, not styles; rules that may help us to attribute meaning to our actions.

When governed by rules, architectural ornament can display its profound connection to cosmos and order. However, the common mistake often made by theorists, historians and practitioners, consists in considering cosmos and order as entirely natural. When Ralph Wornum explains in his *Analysis of Ornament* that the reign of the ornamental begins with the domination of symmetry and contrast over any other considerations, he is actually trying to

ground ornament in the physics and physiology of perception.[24] The same temptation at times pervades Ernst Gombrich's great synthesis on ornament revealingly entitled *The Sense of Order*.[25] Of course, such order depends on a series of natural laws like those that condition the way we perceive forms and colours.[26] Yet, it also appears as a cultural construct.

As a cultural construct, ornament, when governed by clear rules, corresponds both to a historical legacy and to a project, for it is always simultaneously received and transmitted, submitted to preexisting codes and reinterpreted. Rules are essential to allow architecture to connect to its own history in a productive way. The constant negotiation between tradition and novelty presents a political dimension, a juggling between resistance and acceptance. It is after all one of the functions of politics to articulate past, present and future into a coherent perspective.

As we have seen, the architect was also able to express himself through the modulation of rules or codes. Today, pure and boundless variability has replaced modulation. The only alternative to repetition seems to lie in a quest for original solutions, the status of which, work of art or architecture, remains difficult to assess. This constitutes another limit of the discourse on the non-standard.

How can we transpose the lesson of the orders to contemporary digital architecture? A difficulty immediately arises: the crisis of the tectonic is leaving us uncertain about what will eventually replace the conventional elements of architecture if parametric design continues to spread. As Georges Legendre remarks in his *Book of Surfaces*, 'parametric relationships are not parts (…). Thus a form shaped by parametric modulation has no discrete limb to speak of – you cannot chop it into pieces, nor indulge in the separate application of permutation, substitution and scaling of parts.'[27]

In this context, it may be urgent to engage in a reflection, at both theoretical and practical levels, on what may replace parts in a computer-driven design world. Elementary operations such as twisting, bending or folding should probably be envisaged from this perspective, just like certain fundamental types of textures, patterns and topologies. The next stage could be to recognise that these operations – textures, patterns and topologies – can carry a symbolic load. This is already the case with neo-Islamic patterns, which are so often used in projects for the Muslim world. To acknowledge openly their symbolic resonance represents perhaps the best antidote to the return of naive Orientalism. One might even realise that they are not to be systematically associated with a specific culture and the regions where it predominates. The potential meaning of these patterns extends beyond seducing Middle Eastern, Pakistani or Indonesian clients.

At a more fundamental level than cultural and regional connotations, the new regime of relations between the subject and his/her environment could constitute a major source of symbolic inspiration. After all, ornament already conveys essential aspects of this new condition through properties such as tactility.

When looking for rules both rigorous and open to interpretation, the use of the computer offers a unique opportunity. For the first time since the demise of Vitruvian proportions, architecture may be able to reconnect to mathematics in an authentic way.[28] Scripting and algorithmics could be envisaged as a platform on which to base such reconnection, provided that a genuine concern for meaning tempers the quest for innovative programming.

The five orders are not the only source of inspiration which can be mobilised to understand how architectural ornaments can be both abstract and permeated by meaning. Writing may constitute another source of inspiration, not as much in terms of the explicit messages it conveys but because of its intrinsic expressive power. Hebrew, Arabic or Chinese characters talk to us, even if we do not speak the languages. In the lobby of the new city hall of Montpellier in southern France (2011), the architects Jean Nouvel and François Fontès have proposed a new take on the decorative power of writing with a ceiling adorned with photographs of ancient civil-status documents by film director and artist Alain Fleischer.

Having writing in mind may also enable us to take the full measure of the rapidly changing relation between architectural ornament and the body. For the extended and distributed contemporary subject can no longer be approached in terms of proportion and following a model according to which the skeleton represents the main organising principle. We are increasingly made of networks and interfaces, a disconcerting mode of being, which is perhaps better captured by analogy with writing than by more traditional modes of figuration.

Yet, one may wonder whether this mutation will ever come completely true. For part of ourselves also resists such a vision and prefers to stick to a more traditional representation of individuality. We might have no other choice than to alternate between Deleuzian and Cartesian conceptions of the self, between a multiple and distributed and a unified mode of being. In the future, another possible role of architectural ornament could lie in helping us to cope with this double existence without falling into irremediable schizophrenia. More generally, one of the functions of architecture is to help us live multiple lives on various levels, in reality but also in our dreams, as physical beings made of flesh and technology and as fictions fed on desire.

Ornament presents us with a kind of mirror. In this mirror, we see ourselves as we believe we are and as we would like to be. Ornament is inextricably about knowledge and illusion. Although tainted with dreams (but is this not always the case with what is in our mind?), the knowledge component appears essential. After a long eclipse, its role should be on the rise in the near future, once we overcome the limitations of an approach to décor that is almost exclusively based on affect.

We seem now to experience a new ornamental turn, more radical than the one that Kracauer had identified in the 1920s. Kracauer's 'mass ornament' revolved around the property of key collective manifestations of modernity, from labour organisation in Fordist factories to music-hall ballet, to present an ornamental character. Contemporary technological evolution follows an even more spectacular trajectory. In a number of instances, structural approaches yield to interfacing concerns imparted with an ornamental dimension. With its millions of vibrant sites and its billions of colourful pages, the Internet appears less and less as a network of networks; it tends to evoke a sprawling ornament. In early cyberpunk fictions, novelists like William Gibson or Neal Stephenson had evoked virtual worlds resembling some giant Las Vegas Strip.[29] With its shining appearance and irresistible seduction, the Internet has outdone their vision.

Contemporary societies present many ornamental features, which go beyond the decorative character that Cannadine attributed to the British Empire, or the 'surface-level expressions' of the epoch, which attracted the attention of Kracauer during the first half of the 20th century.[30] Cannadine's ornamentalism complemented an aristocratic vision of the world that is no longer sustainable today. As for Kracauer, his mass ornament was made possible by a society composed of relatively anonymous individuals. The age of the mass ornament corresponded to the rise of the undifferentiated crowd. As MIT Media Lab founder Nicholas Negroponte argued as early as the mid-1990s, before the development of online personalised mass consumption,

SENSEable City Laboratory, MIT, Real Time Rome, 2006.
This is a still of an animation displaying the location and intensity of phone calls placed in relation to a concert given by Madonna in Rome. The moving surface is obtained by summing the individual calls placed by the people. Digital technologies enable the passage from individual to collective behaviour and vice versa. The visualisation of real-time urban life evokes contemporary ornamental research.

before the customised recommendations of Amazon and the Apple Store, the digital age would be marked by a strong return of the question of the self: 'in being digital I am *me*, not a statistical subset'.[31] To be more accurate, in the digital age, I am both a statistical subset and myself. In addition to successive phases of Deleuzian dispersion and Cartesian regrouping, contemporary subjectivity seems also characterised by an alternation of anonymity and exacerbated individuation. This new situation gives a sharper relief to the question of ornament. Contemporary ornament is expected to address both masses and highly conscious individuals. Fashion designers like Martin Margiela have bet on this duality.

The age of ornaments meant only for the masses seems to be reaching its end. In a recent book, Lars Spuybroek has suggested a very similar idea.[32] This might account for the re-emergence of architectural décor as a mediating element between the masses and individuals. The political relevance of ornament lies also in this mediating role. To play this role, ornament must convey lessons. Again, it must reconnect with reflection and knowledge.

People want their bodies and lives to be adorned. Institutions and governments develop more and more elaborate design strategies. From Bilbao to New York, and from London to Los Angeles, stararchitects' buildings look like ornaments at the scale of the city. Revealingly, the new dynamic maps produced by research initiatives like the Massachusetts Institute of Technology SENSEable City Laboratory, enable us to follow urban rhythms in real time and to generate ornament-like visualisations.[33] In such a context, the line separating understanding and adornment becomes day after day more permeable. The time has come for architecture to regain its full momentum by throwing some light on what it means to live together in this strange ornamental world.

References

1 I have evoked this transformation in more detail in *Digital Culture in Architecture: An Introduction for the Design Professions* (Basel: Birkhäuser, 2010). On the perspectives opened to designers, see also Paola Antonelli (ed), *Design and the Elastic Mind* (New York: Museum of Modern Art, 2008).

2 William R Shea, *Galileo's Intellectual Revolution: Middle Period, 1610–1632* (New York: Science History Publications, 1977).

3 John G Palfrey, Urs Gasser, *Born Digital: Understanding the First Generation of Digital Natives* (New York: Basic Books, 2008).

4 For an instance of this parallel, see Herbert Muschamp, 'When Ideas Took Shape and Soared', *New York Times*, Friday 26 May 2000, sect B, p 32.

5 Farshid Moussavi and Michael Kubo, *The Function of Ornament* (Barcelona: Actar, 2006).

6 Cf Mario Carpo, 'Ten Years of Folding', in Greg Lynn (ed), 'Folding in Architecture', *Architectural Design* (London, 1993, revised edition London: John Wiley & Sons, 2004), pp 14–19.

7 Gregory Bateson, *Steps to an Ecology of Mind* (San Francisco: Chandler, 1972).

8 See, for instance, Bruno Latour, *We Have Never Been Modern* (Paris, 1991, English trs, Cambridge, MA: Harvard University Press, 1993); Peter Sloterdijk, *Bubbles: Microspherology* (Frankfurt, 1998, English trs, Cambridge, MA, London: Semiotext(e), 2011).

9 Toyo Ito, 'Tarzans in the Media Forest', *2G*, no 2, 1997, pp 121–44, p 132 in particular.

10 Katherine N Hayles, *How We Became Posthuman: Virtual Bodies in Cybernetics, Literature, and Informatics* (Chicago: University of Chicago Press, 1999); Céline Lafontaine, *L'Empire Cybernétique. Des Machines à Penser à la Pensée Machine* (Paris: Le Seuil, 2004).

11 Andrew Benjamin, 'Surfacing the New Sensorium', *Praxis*, no 9, 2007, pp 5–13, p 6 in particular.

12 Sherry Turkle, *Life on the Screen: Identity in the Age of the Internet* (New York, 1995, reprint New York: Touchstone, 1997).

13 Siegfried Kracauer, 'The Mass Ornament', 1926, republished in Siegfried Kracauer, *The Mass Ornament: Weimar Essays* (Harvard: Harvard University Press, 1995), pp 75–88.

14 François Ascher, *La Société Hypermoderne ou Ces Evénements nous Dépassent, Feignons d'en Etre les Organisateurs* (La Tour d'Aigues: Editions de l'Aube, 2005).

15 Margo DeMello, *Bodies of Inscription: A Cultural History of the Modern Tattoo Community* (Durham, North Carolina: Duke University Press, 2000).

16 Jean-François Lyotard, *The Postmodern Condition: A Report on Knowledge* (Paris, 1979, English trs, Minneapolis: University of Minnesota Press, 1984); Fredric Jameson, 'Postmodernism or the Cultural Logic of Late Capitalism', *New Left Review*, I/146, July–

August 1984, pp 53–92, and in particular p 62.

17 This dimension is, for instance, absent from Lars Spuybroek, *The Sympathy of Things: Ruskin and the Ecology of Design* (Rotterdam: V2 Publishing, 2011).

18 See Frédéric Migayrou, Zeynep Mennan (eds), *Architectures Non Standard* (Paris: Editions du Centre Pompidou, 2003); Mario Carpo, *The Alphabet and the Algorithm* (Cambridge, MA: MIT Press, 2011).

19 On performalism see, for instance, Branko Kolarevic, Ali M Malkawi, *Performative Architecture: Beyond Instrumentality* (New York, London: Spon Press, 2005); Yasha Grobman, Eran Neuman (eds), *Performalism: Form and Performance in Digital Architecture* (New York: Routledge, 2012).

20 Oleg Grabar, *The Mediation of Ornament* (Princeton: Princeton University Press, 1992), p 193; Barry Bergdoll, *Karl Friedrich Schinkel: An Architecture for Prussia* (New York: Rizzoli,

1994), p 9.

21 Charles Jencks, George Baird (eds), *Meaning in Architecture* (New York: George Braziller, 1970).

22 Robert Levit, 'Contemporary "Ornament": The Return of the Symbolic Repressed', *Harvard Design Magazine*, no 28, spring/summer 2008.

23 Patrik Schumacher, *The Autopoiesis of Architecture, I. A New Framework for Architecture, II. A New Agenda for Architecture* (London: Wiley, 2011–12).

24 Ralph N Wornum, *Analysis of Ornament, Characteristics of Styles: An Introduction to the Study of the History of Ornamental Art* (London: Chapman & Hall, 1896), p 9.

25 Ernst Hans Gombrich, *The Sense of Order: A Study in the Psychology of Decorative Art* (Ithaca, NY: Cornell University Press, 1979).

26 For a synthesis on this question, see Margaret Livingstone, *Vision and Art: The Biology of Seeing* (New York: Abrams, 2002).

27 Georges L Legendre, *ijp: The Book of Surfaces*

(London: Architectural Association, 2003), pp 2,7.

28 Cf George L Legendre (ed), *Mathematics of Space*, Architectural Design (AD) series (London: John Wiley & Sons), July/August (no 4), 2011.

29 William Gibson, *Neuromancer* (New York: Ace Book, 1984); Neal Stephenson, *Snow Crash* (New York, 1992, reprint New York: Bantam, 2003).

30 Kracauer, *The Mass Ornament*, p 75.

31 Nicholas Negroponte, *Being Digital* (New York: 1995, reprint New York: Vintage Books, 1996), p 164.

32 Spuybroek, *The Sympathy of Things*, p 76.

33 http://senseable.mit.edu/ (accessed on 24 July 2012).

Bibliography

Benjamin, Andrew, 'Surfacing the New Sensorium', *Praxis*, no 9, 2007, pp 5–13.

Buci-Glucksmann, Christine, *Philosophie de l'Ornement. D'Orient en Occident* (Paris: Galilée, 2008).

Canales, Jimena and Andrew Herscher, 'Tattoos and Modern Architecture in the Work of Adolf Loos', *Architectural History*, vol 48, 2005, pp 235–56.

Cannadine, David, *Ornamentalism: How the British Saw Their Empire* (Oxford, New York: Oxford University Press, 2001).

Caye, Pierre, *Empire et Décor: L'Architecture et la Question de la Technique à l'Age Humaniste et Classique* (Paris: Vrin, 1999).

Crinson, Mark, *Empire Building: Orientalism and Victorian Architecture* (New York: Routledge, 1996).

Deleuze, Gilles and Félix Guattari, *A Thousand Plateaus: Capitalism and Schizophrenia* (Paris, 1980, English trs, Minneapolis: University of Minnesota, 1987).

Derrida, Jacques, *Of Grammatology* (Paris, 1967, English trs, Baltimore:

Johns Hopkins University Press, 1976).

Fraenkel, Béatrice, 'Ecriture, Architecture et Ornament: Les Déplacements d'une Problématique Traditionnelle', *Perspective: La Revue de l'INHA*, 2010–11, 1, pp 165–70.

Gleiniger, Andrea and Georg Vrachliotis, *Pattern: Ornament, Structure, and Behavior* (Basel: Birkhäuser, 2009).

Gombrich, Ernst Hans, *The Sense of Order: A Study in the Psychology of Decorative Art* (Ithaca, NY: Cornell University Press, 1979).

Grabar, Oleg, *The Mediation of Ornament* (Princeton: Princeton University Press, 1992).

Gros, Pierre, 'La Notion d'Ornamentum de Vitruve à Alberti', *Perspective: La Revue de l'INHA*, 2010–11, 1, pp 130–6.

Hvattum, Mari, *Gottfried Semper and the Problem of Historicism* (Cambridge: Cambridge University Press, 2004).

Jencks, Charles and George Baird (eds), *Meaning in Architecture* (New York: George Braziller, 1970).

Jones, Owen, *The Grammar of Ornament* (London, 1856, new edition London: Bernard Quaritch, 1868).

Kracauer, Siegfried, *The Mass Ornament: Weimar Essays* (Cambridge, MA: Harvard University Press, 1995).

Levit, Robert, 'Contemporary "Ornament": The Return of the Symbolic Repressed', *Harvard Design Magazine*, no 28, Spring/Summer 2008, pp 70–85.

Llewellyn Nigel, 'Two Notes on Diego da Sagredo', *Journal of the Warburg and Courtauld Institutes*, vol 40, 1977.

Loos Adolf, *Ornament and Crime: Selected Essays* (Riverside, CA: Ariadne Press, 1998).

Lynn, Greg, 'The Structure of Ornament', in Neil Leach, David Turnbull, Chris Williams (eds), *Digital Tectonics* (Chichester, West Sussex: Wiley-Academy, 2004), pp 62–8.

Martin, Reinhold, *The Organizational Complex: Architecture, Media, and Corporate Space* (Cambridge, MA: MIT Press, 2003).

Moussavi, Farshid and Michael Kubo, *The Function of Ornament* (Barcelona: Actar, 2006).

Naginski, Erika, 'Preliminary Thoughts on Piranesi and Vico', *Res. Anthropology and Aesthetics,* no 53/54; Spring/Fall 2008, pp 150–65.

Nègre, Valérie, *L'Ornement en Série: Architecture, Terre Cuite et Carton-Pierre* (Sprimont: Mardaga, 2006).

Negroponte, Nicholas, *Being Digital* (New York: 1995, reprint New York: Vintage Books, 1996).

Payne, Alina, *The Architectural Treatise in the Italian Renaissance: Architectural Invention, Ornament, and Literary Culture* (Cambridge: Cambridge University Press, 1999).

Payne, Alina, *From Ornament to Object: Genealogies of Architectural Modernism* (New Haven, London: Yale University Press, 2012).

Picon, Antoine, *Digital Culture in Architecture: An Introduction for the Design Professions* (Basel: Birkhäuser, 2010).

Reiser, Jesse and Nanako Umemoto, *Atlas of Novel Tectonics* (New York: Princeton Architectural Press, 2006).

Scott, Katie, *The Rococo Interior: Decoration and Social Spaces in Early Eighteenth-Century Paris* (New Haven, London: Yale University Press, 1995).

Spuybroek, Lars, *The Sympathy of Things: Ruskin and the Ecology of Design* (Rotterdam: V2 Publishing, 2011).

Wigley, Mark, *The Architecture of Deconstruction: Derrida's Haunt* (Cambridge, MA: MIT Press, 1993).

Wise, Norton, 'What's in a Line?', in Moritz Epple and Claus Zittel (eds), *Science as Cultural Practice. Vol 1: Cultures and Politics of Research from the Early Modern Period to the Age of Extremes* (Berlin: Akademie Verlag, 2010), pp 61–102.

Wosk, Julie, *Breaking Frame: Technology and the Visual Arts in the Nineteenth Century* (New Brunswick, NJ: Rutgers University Press, 1992).

Index

Figures in italics refer to captions.

A
Abbas, Yasmine 125
Aichi World Expo, Japan (2005): Spanish Pavilion 30
Alberti, Leon Battista 38, 60, 124
Alexander, Christopher 29
Anet, Castle of, France 65
Annales School 14
Antiporda, Alan: *Illusive Photography* 142
Arc-et-Senans saltworks 45, 46, 53
Art Brut 131
Art Nouveau 77, 78, 120
Arts and Crafts Movement 22, 78, 80, 81, 82
Ascher, François 140
Athens: Parthenon 117
Aviler, Augustin-Charles d' 12, 73, 74

B
Baird, George 145
Banham, Reyner 75
Barbaro, Daniele 124
Barcelona, Spain
  Barcelona Universal Exhibition (1929): German Pavilion 20, 21
  Café Torino 120
Baroque 17, 32, 35, 44, 46,
49, 64, 111–12, 117, 122, 125, 126, 134
Bateson, Gregory 136
Bavaria, Germany: Walhalla memorial 117
Beaux-Arts 109
Bechthold, Martin 143
Beijing, China
  National Aquatic Centre (Water Cube), 31, 32
  Olympic Stadium (2008) ('Bird's Nest') 31, 42, 42
Benjamin, Andrew 139
Benjamin, Walter 15, 86
Berlin, Germany
  Altes Museum 108
  Bauakadamie 40, 40, 45
  National Gallery 20
Berlin Physical Society 93–94, 96
Bernini, Gian Lorenzo 46–47, 51, 60, 62, 111, 115
Biberach, Germany: Boehringer Ingelheim Pharmacological Research Laboratories 17, 18, 19
Bilbao, Spain: Guggenheim Museum 26
Bloch, Marc 14
Blondel, François 89, 90
Blondel, Jacques-François 48, 60, 61, 62, 63
Boffrand, Germain 85

Bois-Reymond, Emil du 93, 96
Bordieu, Pierre 51
Bossuet, Jacques-Bénigne 82
Boston, Massachusetts
  Boston Institute of Contemporary Art 31
  Boston Public Library 47
Bosworth, William Welles 107, 108–9, 113
Boullée, Etienne-Louis 45, 53, 59, 66–67
British Empire 121, 122
Brown, Denise Scott 24
Buffalo, New York: Fargo House 87, 88
Bullet, Pierre 104, 104
Bunshaft, Gordon 21, 23
Burges, William 119
Burne-Jones, Edward 81

C
Callimachus 88, 89, 90
Cambridge, Massachusetts
  Harvard Graduate School of Design 143
  Massachusetts Institute of Technology 108
    SENSEable City Laboratory: *Real Time Rome* 154, 155
Canales, Jimena 97
Cannadine, David 121, 122,

153

Cardiff Castle, Wales: the Arab Room *119*
Carlyle, Thomas *78*
Carpeax, Jean-Baptiste
 The Dance 46
 Imperial France Bringing Light to the World and Protecting Agriculture and Science 46, 47, 147
Carpo, Mario *13*
Carroll, Lewis *98*
Caryatid order *148*
Catalan Modernisme 120, *120*
Caye, Pierre *124*
Charles Moore and Perez Architects *147, 151*
Chevrier, Jean-François *42*
Chicago, Illinois
 Aqua Tower *31*
 Chicago Columbian Exposition (1893) *94*
 Illinois Institute of Technology *20*
Choay, Françoise *60*
Choisy, Auguste *39, 39,* 75, *77–78*
City Beautiful Movement *120*
Classicism *93*
Codice Ashburnham *45*
Colberg, Joerg *138*
Cole, Shaun *138*
Composite order *12,* 108, 148
Corinthian order 45, *63,* 64, 88, 89, *90,* 108, 109, *109,* 148
Couchman, Hugh *138*
Croton, Darren *138*

D

Deane, Thomas Newenham *79, 80, 81*
Deerinck, Thomas *137*
Deleuze, Gilles *44, 134, 135*
Delorme, Philibert 65, 66, *67, 73*
Derrida, Jacques *38, 39*
Desgodets, Antoine *63–64*
Detaille, Edouard *126*
Diaz Alonzo, Hernan *53*
Diller, Scofidio + Renfro *31*
Doric order *39, 39,* 44–45, *45, 63,* 64, *94,* 107–8, *107, 109,* 148
Douglas, Evan *17, 19*

Dubai: Marsa Dubai Residential Tower 32, *33*
Duban, Félix *123*
Dublin, Ireland: Kildare Street Club *80, 81*
Durandelle, Louis-Emile *77*

E

Eberswalde Technical School Library, Germany *10,* 17
Eisenman, Peter *43*
Empire style *11*
Enlightenment *83*
Evrard, August *138*

F

Faulders, Thom *141*
Firminy *21*
Fleischer, Alain *152*
Fontaine, Pierre François Léonard *11*
Fontès, François *152*
Foreign Office Architects 19, *19,* 30, 132–33, *136*
Fouquet, Nicolas 110, *112*
Frampton, Kenneth *23,* 75
Francesco di Giorgio Martini *45,* 60, 62
Fréart de Chambray, Roland *90*
French order *12*

G

Galileo Galilei *131*
Gandy, Joseph Michael: *View of the Dome area of John Soane's House looking East 84*
Gang, Jeanne *31*
Gao, Liang *138*
Garnier, Charles *77,* 126, *126*
Gaudi, Antoni *25,* 120
Gautrand, Manuelle *23, 129, 131*
Gehry, Frank *26*
Gerhard, Stephan *138*
Gibson, William *153*
Giedion, Sigfried *55*
Gleiniger, Andrea *19*
Gombrich, Ernst *151*
Gothic Revival style *118,* 122
Grabar, Oleg 9, *50–51,* 125, *145*
Gramazio, Fabio *132*
Gramazio and Kohler 130, *132*

H

Hadid, Zaha 32, *33*
Hagmann, Patric *138*
Hanover Expo 2000, Germany: Dutch Pavilion *148*
Hays, K Michael *43–44*
Heatherwick Studio *132, 134*
Hejduk, John *43*
Helly, John *138*
Helmholtz, Hermann *93*
Hengelo, Netherlands: 3D Garden, Boom Hengelo *148*
Herscher, Andrew *97*
Herzog, Jacques *42*
Herzog & de Meuron *10,* 17, *27, 29, 42, 42,* 132
Hübsch, Heinrich *117*
Hugo, Victor *53*

I

Ionic order 45, *45,* 64, 66, *106, 107,* 108, 148
Istanbul, Turkey: Crimean Memorial Church *119*
Ito, Toyo *137*
Izenour, Steven *24*

J

Jameson, Fredric *141–42*
Jeddah, Saudi Arabia: New Jeddah International Airport *145–46, 147*
Jencks, Charles *24,* 145
Jenkins, Adrian *138*
Jones, Owen 53, *90–91, 91, 92, 94,* 97

K

Kengo Kuma & Associates *149*
Kepes, György *29, 30,* 98
Klein, Ruy: *Klex 1 25*
Klenze, Leo von *106,* 117
Kohler, Matthias *132*
Koolhaas, Rem *13*
Kracauer, Siegfried *140,* 153
Krier, Leon *24–25*
Kubo, Michael 19, *20, 21, 43, 134*

L

LAB Architecture Studio *140*
Labrouste, Henri *47, 52, 53*
Lassay, Marquis de *83*
Latour, Bruno *136*
Laugier, Marc-Antoine *26,*

27, 37
Lausanne, Switzerland:
Connectome Mapping
Toolkit, Ecole Polytechnique
Fédérale de Lausanne and
Université de Lausanne *138*
Le Brun, Charles 111
Le Corbusier 11, 21, *22*, 23,
41, 43, 81, 97, 98
Le Nôtre, André 111, *112*
Le Roy, Julien-David *70*
Le Vau, Louis 111, *112*
Lecce, Italy: Basilica of the
Holy Cross *34*, 35
Ledoux, Claude-Nicolas 45,
46, 53, 59
Legendre, Georges 151
Leicester, England: John
Lewis department store 19,
19, 133, *136*
Lemoyne, Jean-Baptiste *85*
Levit, Robert *19*, 146
Lille, France
  Lille Museum of Modern,
Contemporary and Outsider
Art 23, 129, *131*
  Maison Folie *30*, 31
Lombroso, Cesare *96, 98*
London, England
  British Museum *106*, 108
  Crystal Palace (Great
  Exhibition, 1851) *91*
  Midland Grand Hotel, St
  Pancras train station 118
Loos, Adolf 11, 20, *20*, 23,
37, 48, 71, 96–*97*, 141
Los Angeles, California: Walt
Disney Concert Hall 26
Loti, Pierre 85–86, *86*, 87, 88
Louis XIV, King 49, 110–11,
112, 113
Lynn, Greg *19*, 26, 31, 135
Lyotard, Jean-François 141

M
McKim, Mead & White 47,
53, 108, 109, *109*, 113
Maher, Dennis 87, *88*
Mannerism *64, 65*
Mantua, Italy: Palazzo del
Te *64, 65*
Marble, Scott 26
Margiela, Martin 154
Mariette, Pierre-Jean *67*
Marseilles, France: Unités
d'Habitation 21, *22*
Martin, Reinhold 13

Massé, Jean-Baptiste *113*
Masubichi, Hajime *141*
Mather, Dennis 87
Melbourne, Australia
  Federation Square atrium
  140
  Pixel building 133, *136*
Michelangelo: *Dying Slave*
43, 43
Mies van der Rohe, Ludwig
20, *21*
Minneapolis, Minnesota:
Walker Art Center 29
Modernism, Modernist 9, 10,
12, 14, 15, 16, 20, 23, 24,
24, 25, 46, 47, 53, 54, 59,
71, 72, 75, 77, 81, 86, 87,
87, 90, 97, 98, 99, 103, 122,
125, 145
Modulor Man 21, 98
Montaubon, France *76*
Montpellier, France: city
hall 152
Moore, Charles 147, *151*
Morris, William 80–81, *82*
Moussavi, Farshid 19, *20*, 21,
43, 134
Munich, Germany:
Glyptothek *106*
MVRDV *148*

N
Napoleon I *11*
Napoleon III 46
Natoire, Charles-Joseph *85*
Navarro, Julio *138*
NCMIR/Science Photo Library
137
Negroponte, Nicholas
153–54
neo-classicism *11*, 93
neo-Gothic 32
neo-Romanesque 32
Neutra, Richard 30, *99, 99*
New Haven, Connecticut:
Yale University: Beinecke
Rare Book Library 21, 23, *23*
New Orleans, Louisiana:
Piazza d'Italia 147, *151*
New York City
  AT&T Building *107*, 108–9
  Choice market café,
  Brooklyn *17*, 19
  Columbia University 108
  'Paperless Studio' 26
  Pennsylvania Station 109,
  109

Nouvel, Jean 145, *146*, 152
NOX 30
Nuñez-Yanowsky, Manolo
43, 43

O
Odawara-shi, Japan: Green
Cast *149*
OMA 145–46, *147*
Op art 133
Orientalism 119, *119*, 145,
151
Orlan 139
O'Shea, James 79, *80*, 81
O'Shea, John 79, *80*, 81
Oxford University Museum
of Natural History 79, *80*
Oxman, Neri 130
  Fate Maps 133

P
Palissy, Bernard 66
Palladio, Andrea 60, *63*
Palmer, Harold Sutton *87*
Paris, France
  Bibliothèque Sainte-
  Geneviève 47
  French Ministry of Culture
  28, 29
  Institut du Monde Arabe
  145, *146*
  Louvre Palace *12*
  Flore Pavilion, New
  Louvre 46
  Notre-Dame de Paris *76*,
  78
  Opera *77*, 126, *126*
  police station, 12th
  arrondissement *43, 43*
  Sainte Geneviève Library
  52
  Salon de la Princesse, Hôtel
  de Soubise *85*
  Tuileries Palace 65
Paxton, Joseph *91*
Payne, Alina 64, 97
Peacock, John A *138*
Pearce, Frazer *138*
Percier, Charles *11*
Perez Architects 147, *151*
Perrault, Charles 83, 85
Perrault, Claude *12*, 83, 108
Perrella, Stephen 29
Piranesi, Giovanni Battista
35, *35*, 67, *68, 69, 70, 84*,
85, 92
Postmodernism 13, 24, 25,

50, 122, 145, 147, *151*
Poussin, Nicolas *34–35*
Pozzo, Andrea *125*
Preston Scott Cohen *31, 31*
PTW Architects *31*
PTW Architects, CSCEC +
Design and Arup *32*
Pugin, AWN *53, 80*
Puig i Cadafalch, Josep *120*

R
Racine, Wisconsin: Johnson
Wax Laboratory Tower *21,
23*
Rashid, Hani *26*
Rationalism *75, 78*
Reiser, Jesse *43*
Renaissance *10, 11, 29, 32,
35, 44, 45, 48, 49, 53, 59,
60, 63–66, 73, 82, 86, 91,
106, 111–12, 117, 122, 124*
Rochefort, France: Pierre
Loti's house *85–86, 86*
Rococo *17, 73, 83, 85*
Romanesque *32*
Romano, Giulio *29, 64, 65*
Romanticism *119*
Rome, Italy *49, 50*
  Ara Pacis Augustae, Altar
  of Augustan Peace *44*
  Baths of Caracalla *109, 109*
  Capitol *104*
  Forum of Nerva *105*
  Fountain of the Bees
  46–47, 51
  St Peter's baldachin, St
  Peter's basilica *111, 115*
  Sant'Ignazio *125*
Rossi, Aldo *25, 43*
Rowe, Colin *25*
Ruff, Thomas *10*
Ruskin, John *13, 13, 21,
78–80, 79, 80, 81, 91, 94,
143*

S
Saarinen, Eero *98*
Sabin + Jones LabStudio:
'Branching Morphogenesis'
139
Sagredo, Diego de *60, 60,
62*
St Louis, Missouri:
Wainwright Building *39, 40*
San Francisco, California: De
Young Museum *27, 29, 132*
Sangallo, Giuliano da *36*

Sauerbruch Hutton *17, 18*
Scamozzi, Vincenzo *60, 61,
63, 124*
Schinkel, Karl Friedrich *40,
40, 45, 108, 117, 145*
Schöffer, Nicolas *133*
Scott, George Gilbert *118*
Scott, Katie *73*
Semper, Gottfried *13, 38,
39, 92, 95, 116, 116, 143*
Seoul, South Korea: Galleria
Department Store *129, 130*
Serlio, Sebastiano *63, 64*
Shanghai, China: UK Pavilion,
2010 Expo *132, 134*
Simounet, Roland *21, 23,
131*
Sloterdijk, Peter *61, 66, 136*
Smirke, Robert *106, 108*
Snøhetta *135*
Soane, John *84, 85, 86,
87, 88*
Soler, Frank *28, 29*
Springel, Volker *138*
Spuybroek, Lars *30, 31, 154*
Stelarc *139*
Stephenson, Neal *153*
Studio 505 *133, 136*
Sullivan, Louis *40, 41, 71, 72*

T
Tafuri, Manfredo *54, 67, 70*
Talman, John *111*
Tel Aviv, Israel: Museum of
Art, *31, 31*
Temple of Jerusalem *12*
Thacker, Robert *138*
Thiran, Jean-Philippe *138*
Thomas, Peter *138*
Thouin, Gabriel *115*
Tokyo, Japan: Airspace *141*
Trento, Italy: Palazzo
Roccabruna *110*
Tschumi, Bernard *43*
Turkle, Sherry *139*
Tuscan order *107, 148*
Tverrfjellhytta, Norway:
Norwegian Wild Reindeer
Centre *135*

U
Umemoto, Nanako *43*
UN Studio *129, 130*

V
Vaux-le-Vicomte *110, 112*
Venturi, Robert *24, 25, 147*

Learning from Las Vegas
25
Versailles, France *49, 111,
111*
  Hall of Mirrors *113*
Vicenza, Italy: Teatro
Olimpico *124*
Vienna, Austria: Karlsplatz
metro station *121*
Viennese Secession *120*
Vignola, Giacomo Barozzi da
60, 62, 63
Viollet-le-Duc, Eugène
75–77, 78, 79, 117, 118
Virebent workshop, Toulouse
75, 76
Vitruvius *32, 34, 34, 37,
39, 47, 48, 50, 60, 62, 63,
65, 67, 82, 88–89, 90, 117,
148, 152*
Vrachliotis, Georg *19*

W
Wagner, Otto *120, 121*
Washington DC *49, 122*
Whelan, Edward *79, 80*
White, Simon DM *138*
Wickham Hall, Kent:
Drawing Room *87*
Wiener, Norbert *29, 30*
Wise, Norton *93*
Wittkower, Rudolf *38, 97*
Woodward, Benjamin *79,
80, 81*
Wornum, Ralph *92, 149, 151*
Wren, Christopher *62*
Wright, Frank Lloyd *21,
71, 72*

Y
Yoshida, Naoki *138*

Z
Zimbalo, Giuseppe *34*
Zurich, Switzerland: ETH
Zurich: The Sequential Wall
132

Picture Credits

The author and the publisher gratefully acknowledge the people who gave their permission to reproduce material in this book. While every effort has been made to contact copyright holders for their permission to reprint material, the publishers would be grateful to hear from any copyright holder who is not acknowledged here and will undertake to rectify any errors or omissions in future editions.

Printed in Great Britain
by Amazon